Forty Years in the Academic Trenches

Forty Years in the Academic Trenches

$\diamond$

Change Comes to an American University

Frank Heppner

Ornis Press

Published by Ornis Press
birdman@uri.edu

Other Books by the Author

> *The Seventy Year Train Ride*
> *Railroads of Rhode Island*
> *Teaching the Large College Class*
> *The Green Book of Grading*
> *Islam and Islamic Science*
> *Laboratory Manual in General Biology*
> *Professor Farnsworth's Explanations in Biology*

Documents mentioned herein can be found at the University of Rhode Island library's Special Collections, Manuscripts and Personal Papers office.
https://web.uri.edu/specialcollections/frankheppnerpapers/

Illustrations by Kandis Elliot and Cady Goldfield.

ISBN 978-0-578-72021-0

Heppner, Frank H.
Forty Years in the Academic Trenches: Change Comes to an American University/Frank Heppner/ -1st ed.

Printed in the United States of America
FIRST EDITION

Table of Contents

Preface and Acknowledgments

In 2010, I retired after 41 years of teaching biology at the University of Rhode Island. Recognizing my emeritus status, the university gave me an office and a small amount of lab space in one of the older buildings on campus. I quickly discovered why they had been so generous, in the face of increasing space demands. The building air conditioner had a sound that resembled that of an F-14 taking off from the USS *Enterprise,* if you were standing 50 feet in back of the catapult. The machine had only two positions; off, and afterburner. Fortunately, my hearing was beginning to go, so it wasn't *that* much of a hardship. The room was adequate to my needs, and I *like* aircraft carriers.

A couple of years later, I began to hear rumblings that the building was going to be reassigned, and that the old dudes who had been sequestered there might be on their own. In advance of that possible unpleasantness, I decided to chuck everything I wouldn't want to take to the Home with me when the time came. I had been a compulsive paper saver and had four file cabinets packed full of university correspondence dating back to 1969. I knew that the university library had an archives department and I thought that some future historian might be amused by seeing what day-to-day life at a university like URI was like almost 50 years ago, so I started going through these old files and selecting things I thought might be of interest.

What I found made me alternately recoil in horror and collapse off my chair in laughter. After going through thousands of pieces of paper, I came to two conclusions that scarcely can be challenged:

Nothing has changed.
Everything is different.

Nothing has changed because the things we professors complained about half a century ago have not fundamentally been addressed. Everything is different because the way we do things has been dramatically altered by university economics, the nature of the student body, the research environment, increased bureaucratization. Ad infinitum.

So I decided to go a little further and not just send the library boxes of papers, but some editorial comments to put the papers in perspective. Then, my having written a couple of books, the comments somehow morphed themselves into book form, intended to be read both by university administrators, and new and old faculty both at URI and elsewhere.

What started out to be a simple recollection ended up being a commentary on institutional constipation, which has been described as the tendency of bureaucracies to continue practices long beyond their usefulness, and in some cases even beyond any institutional memory of why they started in the first place. I want to state straight out that this is a narrative, not a scholarly book (not that there's anything wrong with scholarly books). Although I have described my experiences at the University of Rhode Island, I suspect old-timers at any reasonably large college or university could tell a similar tale.

When I finished the manuscript for this book, I showed it to my wife, who is a retired psychologist, and a very good editor.

"Well, it was interesting and all that, and I learned a lot, but I had one question by the time I finished."

"What's that?"

"If URI was such a nest of vipers, and academia became so corrupt, why did you stay there for forty years? You had quite a few other opportunities."

I was stopped in my tracks. She was right. You didn't have any feeling from the manuscript about why a college professor could have a wonderful life, and what would keep you plugging as you had routine encounters with maddening bureaucrats. So I decided to address this issue by including short chapters from time to time (that I call, forgive me, "Chapterlets") about times in my life that directed me into science and the professorate, beginning with the earliest days, to give a bit of balance.

The statements in this document reflect my own opinions, and are not those of the University of Rhode Island, nor the Rhode Island Board of Education. The original documents referred to here are in the archives of the University of Rhode Island. I thank Sarina Rodrigues of the University of Rhode Island Library for help with the archives, and my wife Marjorie Heppner for copy editing. Kandis Elliot generously volunteered to format the manuscript. Harold Pomeroy, Evan Preisser, Mike Heppner, William Croasdale, and Jeff Sack graciously read early versions. However, any mistakes are mine alone.

Chapter 1
In the Beginning

I grew up in San Francisco, a fourth-generation Californian. I had never been east of Denver, aside from a dreadful 1958 freshman year at Rensselaer Polytechnic in Troy, New York. The rest of my higher education was spent in West Coast state institutions; Berkeley, San Francisco State, Davis, and the University of Washington. I vaguely knew that America's Founding Fathers had lived someplace on the East Coast, but that was about the end of my knowledge and interest in the Northeast.

In 1969, my first wife and I were finishing post-doctoral scientific research positions in Seattle. She was an immunologist and I was an ornithologist. I had a chance to teach a big introductory course at University of Washington, and to my amazement loved it. However, as the end of our two-year appointments drew near, it became time to look for permanent academic positions.

On the face of it, this shouldn't have been too much of a challenge. There were actually science faculty shortages, in those days of the science and space races with the Soviet Union. Lingering memories of the hydrogen bomb existed, and scientists were the new front-line troops. We started looking at the traditional time—the fall semester of the year before you wanted to start. But two-professional families were very unusual, and there was no affirmative action. So, I'd hear about an opening somewhere, but there would be nothing for her. Then she'd hear about something, and there would be no possibility for me. We bounced around like this all during the fall of 1968, and into the first couple of months of 1969. By March, thoroughly discouraged, we decided that we'd jump at the next opening, whoever it was for, and the other one would sell cars or go door-to-door.

However, in early March, which was very, very late in the academic hiring season (which should have raised some alarm bells, but what did we know then?), an advertisement in *Science* appeared for a regular, tenure-track faculty appointment at the University of Rhode Island in the Department of Zoology to start in the Fall semester of 1969. The specialty field was open, which again was unusual for the time. It just said the candidate would be expected to teach a large introductory biology course and conduct research in his (yes, it was "his" in those days) specialty.

I knew nothing about the University of Rhode Island, so I asked my post-doc adviser, Don Farner, who was a member of the National Academy of Sciences, about it. He suggested I not apply. Why? He said that URI was a great place to begin one's career, but a terrible one to try to continue it. How come? He said that Rhode Island was a blue-collar industrial state, where the rich WASPS sent their kids to Brown or out-of-state, the rich ethnics like the Italians or Irish sent their kids to the Catholic Providence College or Boston College, and the whole idea of outstanding public universities, like UCLA or Michigan was basically foreign in Rhode Island and didn't generate a lot of voter support. The smaller New England state universities were the places where the machinist's kid could learn to be an accountant. There were enough resources to get a new, young faculty member going, but the state simply wouldn't spend the kind of money needed to promote a high-level academic career. In retrospect, I now understand why Farner was a member of the National Academy.

However, by this time we were not in a position to quibble. I never did make a hiring visit. I got the job on the basis of a single phone interview (which should have made me *very* nervous). Once I took the job and we moved to Rhode Island, my first wife's Seattle post-doc advisor called a guy he knew at the Brown medical school in Providence ("I know a guy," is the official *modus operandi* of the State of Rhode Island), and they *made* an Assistant Professor of Medicine position specifically for her—not possible today with Affirmative Action. So within a couple of months we were both employed at jobs we were educated to do. The only difference was that she got paid a lot more, and Brown was more prestigious than URI.

My job application consisted of a single page cover letter. Attached was a CV, three references, a couple of my papers—and that was it. Today, you need a truck to hold the supporting documentation for an academic job application.

Chapterlet 1 · The Kid Scientist

I was born in 1940. My father was a doctor, which didn't mean the same thing economically then as it does now. People spoke of "The doctor's Buick," or "The doctor's Dodge," rather than her Mercedes or BMW. We lived in a three-unit apartment on Russian Hill, now very posh, but then part of the Italian North Beach. Our downstairs neighbor was a hardware salesman, and our upstairs neighbors were rich, reflecting the heterogeneous nature of the neighborhood. That upstairs Hester and Irving were rich was confirmed when I later found out they owned a Pieter Brueghel the Younger painting. They had no children, and I soon found that I could turn that to my advantage, inasmuch as any five-year-old can make plans.

There has been an argument about whether scientists are born or made. I can say definitively, "Either or both." Time and time again, I have had good fortune in my life simply because I was at the right place at the right time. Hester loved kids, and used any excuse to have contact with me. Like many children of my generation, I was an early reader (around 3) because my parents taught me and used some of the early alphabet toys. Mine was a Cressco, from 1940. By the time I was 5 I knew enough science so that when Hester made fudge using Ghirardelli chocolate (whose factory was a few blocks away), she could bribe me to come upstairs and I would expound on planetary moons in return for a plateful of fudge.

I joined the California Academy of Sciences Student Section in San Francisco when I was 10, and it was a haven, because it was filled with others of my own kind. In truth, I think we kid geeks were politically and socially more adept than our present day counterparts and we weren't hassled as much as non-athletic kids appear to be today.

As an example of opportunities we made for ourselves, I still have my first science class lesson plan. It is dated May 2, 1952, and it was about reptiles. I was in 6th grade, which was elementary school in those days, and I was 11. Mrs. Smith, my 6th grade teacher loathed and was afraid of science, although she was wonderful in other areas. Being a helpful kid, I overcame my shyness (ha) and volunteered to teach the science part of class for her. She accepted gratefully. Hard to imagine that happening today.

As you read this, you are probably thinking, "Yeah, right! If he had really done that he would have been made into a paté after school by the other boys." Under normal circumstances, I would agree, but by a strange coincidence, in the early part of the semester, I had made friends with a neighbor kid named Gary, who was built like Arnold Schwarzenegger when he was 12, and liked to hike as I did. I providentially helped him with his homework, and he served as my bodyguard. Sometimes geeks need a little assistance to carry on their activities.

It was kind of eerie for me as I read this scrap of paper over, because I could already see some of the techniques I later used to keep the attention of disinterested students: (1) Gross them out. "In the US, the rattle-snake is used for food; it is a delicacy which is packed in cans as snake steaks. It has a shrimp or chicken flavor." (2) Give them credit for things that may not be true—a little flattery never hurts. "What is a reptile? That is a question many of us have asked one time or another." (3) Give a lot of demonstrations. "Today I have brought along a few living specimens. The first specimen is a common fence lizard. Some people call them blue-bellies." (4) Include notes to yourself. "(Bring out tripod magnifier and shorty microscope)." (5) Encourage participation. "You are all invited to come up and see these reptiles and amphibians in their native habitat.—Please do not feed the animals." (6) Acknowledge assistance. "The wild beasts were caught with the help of Fred Bellero, who also helped in the construction of the aquarium and the terrium(sic). My thanks to him."

The final line in the script I can't believe I actually said; it does reflect my level of confidence. Even my bodyguard wouldn't have been able to help me if I'd delivered this one:

"Next week, you should be so lucky, I will talk about electricity."

I find no record of a hospital visit around this time, so I guess I was sensible and didn't say it.

Later, in high school, the tables were turned, and some of my teachers dealt with my overconfidence in a somewhat different way.

You are all invited to come up and see these reptiles and amphibians in their native habitat.--- Please do not feed the animals.

Next week, you should be so lucky, I will talk about electricity'

High school sophomore English teacher encourages me
to give the next oral presentation.

number.

We just finished studying rocks
and minerals and we are continu-
ing with the subject of weather.
We have Frank Heppner telling us
something about it each day,
which we think is very interesting to listen to.

Art period has been a lot of
fun. We have been fingerpainting
with two colors. By using your
finger, side of your hand, the palm
of your hand or your arm or elbow make very pretty designs.
When the picture is finished it
can be mounted.

Reporter: Sharon McCrary.

For a new hire in a department with megaclasses, being asked to teach one was emotionally like being asked to give a seminar in the La Scala opera house.

Chapter 2
Teaching a Megaclass

Although no one discussed it with me directly, discreet inquiry after I showed up at URI soon revealed the general story about why I had been hired on such short notice. It seemed that there had been a disputed denied-tenure case in the department that had started a couple of years back, and the denied prof had been replaced in his big required Freshman class with a distinguished elderly professor who had been brought out of retirement specifically to teach the course. However, by the beginning of 1969, he was showing signs of candidacy for assisted living, and by February it was clear that he wasn't going to be able to teach the big class in the fall and would need to be replaced. Today, there would be hordes of potential temporaries available, but at the time they were non-existent. The department used the disputed guy's tenure track line to hire me. If he had later won his case, I would have been in a bit of a pickle. I didn't get the whole story until years later.

One might assume that the first class given to a new university faculty hire might be an upper division course in the rookie's specialty, enabling him or her to phase into an activity that was probably brand new, other than a stint or two as a teaching assistant. Alas, that is not the way it usually works.

The first class I taught at URI in 1969 had more than 900 students. It was Biology 2, required for every student in the university except those majoring in Biology and related fields, who took a different majors-oriented course. Imagine the effrontery of saying all college graduates *needed* to know something about Biology! There were similar specific course requirements for everyone in English composition, math, and a few others. There was no escape for students from these requirements. Needless to say, not all the enrollees in Biology 2 were happy campers.

Courses like Bio 2 were the most challenging in the university for anyone who wanted to do a halfway decent job of teaching. You had arcane, complex subjects to explain to mobs of unmotivated and even hostile students, plus you essentially managed a small business, with accounting, budget, personnel, customer relations, and quality control concerns. The training that universities normally asked new faculty to have in these areas was—zero. As long as you had a Ph.D. from a name school, and were off to a running start in research, you were good to go. The situation is a LITTLE different now, but not much.

This was much like what would happen if, on her first surgical rotation, a second-year medical student suddenly heard the Chief Surgeon say, "Welcome to your first operation, Ms. Jones! This is going to be a quadruple bypass in a 78-year-old patient with pneumonia. I know you've read about the procedure in your coursework, and to show our confidence in you, the other surgeons and I are going to leave the O.R. now, grab a cuppa Joe, and you can do the procedure by yourself. The nurses are very competent. Have a good time; we'll be back in a couple of hours." Would that be acceptable in medicine? Probably not, but it is the norm in university education.

In addition to the giant Bio 2, I also taught a graduate seminar. In the second semester of my first year, I taught Bio 2 again, and in addition a two-lab-section upper division course, and a different grad seminar. The following year, I added a two-lab-section upper division course in the fall semester, for a total of 5-6 classes a year, two of them huge ones. That was considered a normal teaching load for new science faculty. Young faculty today have asked me how on earth I got any research done, let alone handle the administrative work of courses before we had personal computers, which didn't come along until the '80s. They are invariably startled when I tell them that it was much easier for faculty before computers, and in my case, even before copy machines. The reason is simple. The department employed a huge number (in today's terms) of support staff.

In 1969, my department had 18 faculty members. In addition, the Chair had a personal secretary, there were two general secretaries, a fiscal clerk, a department handyman, a stockroom clerk, a departmental photographer, a departmental artist, a microscope and instrument technician, an animal caretaker, and a small army of student office and lab helpers and gofers. Each big course had a professional lab manager (not a grad student), and teaching loads were modest for the teaching assistants.

Exams required a lot of preparation, both then and now, but here's how exams worked back in the day. You'd type out, or write out in longhand, your multiple-choice questions for the exam (you could also dictate it, which many faculty preferred). You gave it to the department secretary, who typically had a master's degree in English. She (always a "she" in those days) would copy edit it, type a clean copy, and return it to you for approval. If it was okay, she would give it to one of the lower level secretaries to type onto a "stencil." You had to be a pretty good typist (certainly better than most faculty) to prepare one of these, because corrections were difficult. Once the stencil was made, the exams were printed off by office staff using the "mimeograph machine." This was before Xerox. The finished exams were collated, stapled, and delivered by the secretary to your lab coordinator, who brought them to the exam venue.

When the students took the exams, they entered their answers on a "punch card," something that looked like the old IBM computer cards, but you had a little stylus, and punched a hole in the card to indicate your answer to each question. These were used until very recently in elections, of "hanging chad" infamy. When the exam was over, the stack of cards was delivered to the microscope technician, who had a little machine that read the card, and showed the number correct on a dial. The technician would call out the student's name and score to a teaching assistant who had already entered the students' names in the "green book," a spiral bound notebook that contained students' names and spaces for scores. The two would use a call-and-response system like airline pilots and controllers, to make sure there were no errors and in fact, the system was almost foolproof. Another TA drew the curve and made an answer key for posting. At the end of about 3 hours, all the exams were corrected, a mean was calculated, a curve drawn, and a key posted (students were encouraged to copy their answers on their question sheets, which they kept after the exam). Today, the total turn-around time for computer-corrected exams is often much longer.

Total faculty time for large class instructors in these essentially mechanical administrative tasks? Zero.

In the late '80s when faculty started being issued personal computers, we were ecstatic. We believed Steve and Bill's advertising that these gadgets were "labor-saving devices." In actuality, from an administrative standpoint they were labor-transferring devices, whereby secretarial and low-level technical work could now be shifted to faculty, who weren't skilled enough to do these things before the computers. They didn't need to get raises as a result of this extra menial work, and the support personnel could be canned. Now, my old department has a fiscal clerk and a secretary/receptionist—that's it. No wonder the administration was so happy to buy computers. Although the personal computer greatly increased the number of things I could do in both teaching and research, it also increased my mindless busywork by 5–10 hours a week.

Chapter 3
Solidarity Forever

Relatively few little kids say, "When I grow up I want to be a college professor." Over time, a child might discover a strong interest, say chemistry or history, and find that you could actually make a living at it by becoming a professor. Along the way, he or she might discover that there might be ancillary benefits to professordom. One of the attractions of academia to me, before I actually took my first job, was that you could be a rugged individualist, while at the same time drawing a paycheck whose size, at least in part, was dependent on how good a job you did. It did not take me long when I came to URI to find out that not all my colleagues shared this view.

Recall that this was 1969. The influence of the '60s was still strong (except the peace and love part); cities were burning, civil disobedience was everywhere, and the Student Movement was daily growing in influence. Woodstock promoted peace and love, a feeling that lasted a couple of months until Altamont. On campus, the political left was dominant among the faculty, just as the outside world suspected. Against this background, there was a union movement developing in the professorate.

At URI, the lead organizer for a faculty union was the American Association of University Professors (AAUP). It was not a universally popular movement. The faculty was rather sharply divided along disciplinary lines. The sciences and engineering wanted no part of a union. They LIKED the idea that they could bargain individually for their contracts. In fairness, many of these faculty had options other than academia in industry or government where they could appropriately use their education and skills. On the other hand, if you loved Elizabethan Poets, there weren't many big Renaissance English factories out in Dubuque that you could go to if opportunities were limited at your university. So, the humanities and many of the social sciences were generally in favor of unionization.

In retrospect, the pro-union folks were much better at campus politics than were the scientists and engineers, which is why faculty unions eventually became almost universal. When years later I was drafted, at gunpoint as it were, to serve on the faculty senate, it appeared at the meetings that the folks in Poly Sci and Economics LOVED the parry and thrust of legislative debate, while the science folks brought their lab notebooks to work on between votes.

11

So, there were bitter discussions and division on campus. I went to a union organizing meeting, just to see what it was all about. It was like a time warp. Here were all these middle-aged, middle-class professors in their tweed jackets with leather elbow patches singing Woodie Guthrie dust bowl songs from the '30s. The leaders were ecstatic. This was the Worker-Student Alliance come to life! Right at URI!

The union organizers eventually won. You didn't have to join the union, but if you didn't, an amount equal to the union dues was taken from your salary and given to the union—a not uncommon practice. Along with a number of others, I objected to this philosophy. The argument was that everyone benefited from a union, so everybody should pay for the benefits. On the other hand, in a university, many individuals, especially those who had gained some degree of academic celebrity, would be able to do BETTER than the union contract, and it was adding insult to injury to ask these individuals to fund an organization that was costing them money. This was like having to tip the hangman to make sure the knot was tied correctly. Considerably later, contracts were modified to allow exceptions for academic superstars.

Being an arrogant young puppy, I considered myself as part of that class, and wrote a letter to the state controller in 1973, objecting to the listing of mandatory union dues as a "voluntary" contribution on our paycheck stubs. Needless to say, this did not endear me to my colleagues in the English department, but my recent acquisition of tenure may have given me a certain amount of confidence.

In 1979, the AAUP staged a strike and set up picket lines. Needless to say, I was vehemently against a strike, viewing it as unfair to students who had already paid their tuition. Faculty were urged to honor the picket lines, and this led to an incident that is one of my fondest memories. A picket line was set up between my parking lot and my classroom building. As I approached the line and it was clear that I intended to walk through it, the screaming and yelling started. One of the union leaders, a brilliant far-left lawyer, debater, and union organizer named Elton Rayack from the Economics Department got in my face. It was clear that he was having the time of his life, in league with his heroes, the longshoremen and teamsters. I, however, just wanted to get to my class. We were JUST at the point of exchanging blows when somebody separated us, and with as much dignity as I could muster I marched past the line and into the building, the jeers following me. That was as close as I got to a fistfight in my entire adult life. At the time, I thought I could have cleaned Elton's clock, but I later found out he had been a successful amateur boxer, so the fates were smiling at me. After all the union dust settled, we became colleagues again, and I loved to see Elton debate. He could have beaten Johnny Cochrane if he were still in court.

In retrospect, having a faculty union at URI was probably a good thing. Those of us in the sciences and engineering could still augment our salaries in an individual way through grants and research contracts, and the salaries for the humanities folks, who are the soul of any decent university, went from embarrassingly low to passable.

Lest the intrepid reader think I was an isolated whiner about the establishment of a faculty union at URI in the '70s, an anti-union letter and petition I composed, then sent to then-President Frank Newman, and AAUP head Gino Silvestri might offer some perspective. I circulated the petition to the Zoology, Oceanography, and Electrical Engineering departments. Over 90% of each department signed in support. I suspect that had I circulated the petition in, say, Political Science, it would have been used to start the cheery bonfire surrounding the pole to which I had been affixed. For my own warmth and protection, of course.

Some of the comments on the petition form were illuminating. "I bring in 4x my salary—for what?" "The philosophy and procedure of the union is most objectionable to me." Perhaps most vigorous was, "AAUP and admin are engaged in a power struggle, which distracts both sides from the real purpose of a university. I see collective bargaining as collective greed, and I see the administration as preoccupied with economics to adhere to the budget that a cheapskate legislature (and citizenry) has given us. Mediocrity pervades all, not just the AAUP." So there. It appears that some of the problems administration and faculty have to deal with today have been in play for at least three, and maybe four decades.

A statement in the petition deserves explication. "There is some confusion about the state of the employment market for academics. Whereas it is true that it is very difficult for new Ph.D.'s to find favorable conditions for employment, there is considerable mobility among established, excellent faculty." For decades, various interested parties have created the impression that there is a shortage of scientists in the United States, and therefore massive programs are needed to encourage more students to acquire Ph.D.'s in science. Agencies particularly vigorous in this view have been the National Science Foundation and the National Institutes of Health. Let's take a look at this.

In the 1960s, there WAS a shortage of scientists and engineers, fueled by the cold war with the Soviet Union. I finished my Ph.D. in 1967, and this was just about the beginning of the end of the boom. By 1975, when the petition was written, it was starting to enter public consciousness that "it is very difficult for new Ph.D.'s to find favorable conditions for employment."

One of the reasons for this was the tremendous overbuilding in the sciences in American universities during the '60s due to the Cold War. By the end of the '60s, the American military had pretty much discovered much of the critical scientific information they needed about the ocean and space, and university defense spending started to dry up. However, the universities had tremendously ramped up their capacity to turn out new scientists. Before long, there was a glut.

The reason for the surplus is pretty simple. There are only about 400 universities in the US that maintain big-time research programs that produce and hire lots of Ph.D.'s. Industry tends to employ Ph.D.'s in a limited number of highly specialized areas. There were 4,298 degree granting, post-secondary institutions in the U.S. as of the 2017–2018 school year, according to the National Center for Education Statistics. If a newly minted Ph.D. ends up working today in a school that is NOT one of the favored 400, the probability that he or she will ever continue his or her research in a significant way is small; they're going to teach. But graduate education in science until recently provided little to no formal instruction in teaching.

Okay, so does the supply of newly-minted Ph.D.'s match the number of research level academic jobs? In 2016, 12,627 Ph.D. degrees in biological sciences were awarded by American graduate schools. For my part, I turned out 5 Ph.D.'s in my career, which is a VERY low number. It is more typical that a researcher at a major university will turn out 20–30 Ph.D.'s. So in my case, there was one to replace me when I retired, and the other four went—? They didn't go to places like URI. They went to 4-year colleges where they became primarily teachers. That, however, is not why they got their Ph.D.'s. They prepared for, and wanted to be researchers. In academic science, the US now turns out far more Ph.D.'s than can be employed at "grade A" research institutions or industry. This is one of the reasons there are so many newly-minted science Ph.D.'s floating around universities, eager to accept low-pay adjunct jobs, or decades-long post-docs.

So professional science is more like film acting than school teaching. A few scientists get to be stars, and command research empires at Harvard, or Google, or Cal Tech. The vast majority teach at community or four-year colleges; something the new Ph.D.'s mostly didn't want to do and didn't prepare for.

So why does the system crank out far more new grads than the system needs? Mainly because full-time faculty researchers need grad students to help with our research. The HONEST thing to say to a new grad student interested in research is to tell them at the outset that research is like rock or movie stardom. "Very few who start out wanting it, make it. But, if you think you're going to be the one, more power to you, and I'll do what I can to help you. But no guarantees." Unfortunately, that little speech is not given often enough.

The flip-blade knife that Jack Savage
carried actually belonged to me, after I got
it in the Philippines.

Chapter 4
The Decline of Eccentricity

When I finished my scientific training in the late '60s, a reasonably bright young scientist could go either into industry/government or academia, much as he or she can today. However, industry was perceived as a hive for personality deficient corporate drones, the "Man in the Grey Flannel Suit" of IBM legend, or Riesman's "Lonely Crowd." If you were a child of the '60s, you wanted to do your own thing, and a university was just the place to do it.

As a Berkeley graduate of 1962, the choice for me was clear. However, I did not realize how insular the University of Rhode Island was at the time. I was the first faculty member in the Zoology Department to have received his Ph.D. from a graduate institution *west of the Hudson River.* And I had been an undergraduate at Moscow West, as Berkeley was known in certain quarters.

However, once I settled in, I discovered that this "differentness" was precisely the reason that I had been hired so easily. The young bucks in the rapidly expanding and ambitious URI Zoology department had decided that they wanted to compete on a larger playing field than New England state universities historically had, and they actually thought they were going to be able to mop up the floor with Brown University, which they perceived as old, fusty, and stodgy. So, fresh different blood. Ah, the sweet naivety of youth.

Having discovered that URI's perception of Berkeleyites was that we were oversexed, drug fiend radicals, I had a certain reputation to live up to, and I didn't want to disappoint. As I hadn't done a hiring seminar, I gave some thought to the first department seminar I would give once I was established. I decided not to talk about my post-doc work, fascinating as it was, but a new field that I thought was tremendously exciting, especially as Neil Armstrong had stepped on the moon only a few months before. So I decided to give a review paper on exobiology, or the investigation of the possibility of extraterrestrial life, which was very trendy, and was becoming a "respectable" scientific field, with the advent of Project Ozma in 1960, and NASA's establishment of the SETI program in 1972. I had been a rabid amateur rocketeer as a teenager (something wildly improbable today, due to safety concerns), so this came naturally to me.

The usual point of these department seminars was to bring in outside experts. Well, if I was going to talk about alien life, why not give the seminar as an alien life form? With the cooperation of the department chair, I kept out of sight until seminar time, and walked in as a full-dress alien. One of the most senior members of the department (Yale and ex-Navy), sitting in the front row, bit his pipe stem in half. It was a wild success.

I followed this with similar eccentricities in my teaching. My maxim was that, with respect to students, if you don't have their attention you can't teach them, and I was shameless about getting their attention.

At the opening lecture of my giant general bio class, I wore a three-piece suit, conservative tie, shiny shoes, and a pocket watch with chain. The second lecture followed suit. However, two sessions after the first lecture, I drove a motorcycle into the class's auditorium, dressed as an outlaw biker, with "Born to be Wild" playing on the PA. Why? The topic of the lecture was, "What's the difference between something that's alive, versus something that is not alive?" The vast majority of the students had looked at this question in high school biology, where they were given a list to memorize of characteristics that distinguished between alive or not, like respiration, excretion, etc. The biker, whose stage name was Jack Savage, explained to the class that he LOVED his bike. But how could you love a "thing?" He pointed out that you could love something that wasn't human, like a dog. But a motorcycle? He then explained his insight. Before he was invited to be a high school dropout, he took a biology class, and had to memorize a list of characteristics of living things. Living things require energy. Living things respond to stimuli, etc. Then it hit him. His bike had the characteristics of living things, therefore the bike was alive, thus he could love it. But he couldn't be sure he remembered everything, so he thought he'd drop by a biology class where there were a lot of experts.

He then went down the list. Living things respire. He pointed out the bike's air cleaner. Living things require energy. He pointed to the gas cap. He came up with six or seven characteristics of living things, then asked for the class's help. Maybe he forgot some. Hands went up all over the auditorium. One by one, he showed that the bike had the characteristic that the student came up with. Then came the clincher. The bike couldn't reproduce.

That stumped him. By no stretch of the imagination could he imagine how the bike could reproduce itself. If he parked his bike next to a Yamaha in the garage, and came back six months later, there wouldn't be a bunch of little

Mo-Peds scooting around the floor. But then he said that observation made him very sad. By now, class participation was widespread. Remember, this was 900 students in a classroom with a balcony. Some student invariably asked, "*Why* does that make you sad?" He replied, "Because I'm gonna have to go down to the convent and tell sister Maria Theresa that she ain't alive, because she ain't never gonna reproduce!" Pandemonium. Then he asks the class, "So that's it? If you don't have the *natural* capacity to reproduce, you're not alive?" Silence. They know there has to be something wrong, but nobody knows what. He then pulls a roll of cash out of his pocket, holds it up and says, "I will give this $10,000.00 to anybody who can produce for me the son or daughter of a mule. All mules are born sterile. According to you, then, mules can walk, pull a plow, and crap, but they ain't alive." Pandemonium again. There then followed a more-or-less straight lecture that introduced the questions of when to pronounce someone legally dead, and the question of defining death in an AI robot. This lecture was aimed primarily at the premeds and nurses in the class, because the question of the definition of life and death was becoming a popular issue in the press, and medical folk were in the center of the discussion.

Professor Doktor Viktor Alucard of the Bucharest Institute of Hematology offers to do diagnostic work on the blood of one of my first-year biology class teaching assistants.

I also gave a Halloween lecture on the "Biological Basis of Myth and Legend" dressed as Count Dracula, who was carried into the lecture in a coffin borne by my teaching assistants. There then followed an absolutely straight historico-medical lecture about the likely biological source of stories about werewolves, vampires, the Loch Ness monster, etc. The later Evolution lecture was given by Thomas Huxley, speaking for Charles Darwin.

However, as my career as a large class lecturer drew to a close, I began to notice a not-so-subtle shift in the students. Instead of viewing these "character" presentations as a welcome break from the demanding and technical routine lectures, and responding with laughter, applause, and participation, the students would become nervous. Class participation plummeted. This wasn't on the syllabus. How could you take notes? What would be on the exam? Where was the Powerpoint? Sadly, I realized that the times, they had a'changed, and post-retirement life was becoming more attractive.

And for faculty, there was a complete turnaround in the acceptance of eccentricity in academia versus industry. Now, if you're smart and want to be weird, you work for a startup software company. University full-time science faculty appear to be currently viewed by university administration as single-purpose, grant-getting machines, and any activity that departs from the driven pursuit of overhead money is frowned upon. In later chapters, we will explore why this might have happened, and why recent developments may have changed things a bit.

The author as Thomas Huxley, defending Charles Darwin's Theory of Evolution. The idea for this lecture was "borrowed" from Berkeley's Richard Eakin lecture on Darwin, where Eakin appeared AS Darwin.

Chapterlet 2 · The Teen Years

This book is about changes in higher education, but there has been a parallel change in how kids interested in science navigate their way through the educational system. When I was a sub-teen and teen in San Francisco, the major science museums and many high schools had after-school and Saturday programs for "young scientists." There were adults associated with these programs, but they were basically there to find resources for the kids—like cars for field trips, and access to the scientists in the museum for help with projects.

I recently did an online search for this kind of kid program, but I couldn't find a single one that was like the old ones that were in the California Academy of Sciences, the Randall Junior Museum, and the Lux Electronic Labs in San Francisco. There are still youth science programs, but they seem to be primarily concerned with showing kids who have little interest in science that "science is fun" and have structured programs that let kids touch baby sharks in tanks, build robots from kits, and play with virtual reality gadgets. A far cry from providing terrariums where your tarantulas collected on recent field trips could be stored, or introducing you to the Curator of Entomology to see if you really did discover a new species of bee—when you were 13.

The most influential of these programs for me was the Student Section of the California Academy of Sciences, now defunct. There was a Junior Section for kids up to the age of 13, and a Senior section for 14–18. There was an adult "Director" but we hardly ever saw him. The place was really run by the Seniors, who designed and gave the lectures, arranged and accompanied the field trips, and helped the Juniors with their projects. A stunning number of young folks went on to distinguished scientific careers. Peter Raven became the Director of the Missouri Botanical Garden and the author of a best-selling biology textbook. Terry Trosper got her Ph.D. in biophysics from Berkeley and went on to be a world authority on the preservation of paper in antique books. Tom Briggs got a Ph.D. in chemistry from Berkeley, discovered one of the standard oscillating chemical reactions used in chem labs everywhere, and at the same time became the head of Chemistry at Lowell high school in San Francisco, and an Associate Curator of Entomology at the Cal. Academy. Not bad for no adult participation, eh? This might be contrasted with present-day, litigation-wary science programs for kids that view risk-containing activities with horror.

A modern education bureaucrat and her lawyer friends would be shocked to the point of fainting to see how much freedom science geeks were allowed in the '50s. I went to Polytechnic High School, which basically provided preparation for the skilled trades, but had a small college prep program. This was when the space program was big, and everyone was afraid that the Russians would build better rockets than we could. A small group of kids in the electronics lab got together and decided to build rockets themselves. The original group was Phil Marquis, Fred Stark, Valerie Ford, Bob Miller, Dawn Hollander and myself (yes, there were two girls). Later, Tom Briggs from the Cal. Academy student group joined us. We had no school sponsorship or adult supervision, but the teachers often gave us resources for our independent after-school activity. The Randall Junior Museum let us use their machine shop. Our high school chem teacher let us test our explosive rocket fuel in the chem lab fume hoods after school (I can just imagine the blanched look on the face of a modern high school chem teacher if she received such a request). We called ourselves the Bay Cities Rocket Society, BCRS. I kept in touch with all of them over the years. Fred became the Chair of the Physics Department in the best high school in San Francisco. Bob became an Episcopal priest who liked to work with indigenous people in the jungles of South America, Phil became a plant manager for Litton Industries. Valerie became a pioneer in the use of computers for health statistics and did very well for herself, Dawn was the only one I lost track of, and I became a professor and world traveler. I believe that much of our later success is due to the skills we had to teach ourselves, independent of adult supervision, in BCRS.

Members of the Bay Cities Rocket Society working on rocket parts in a museum machine shop. All the people in the picture went on to careers in science.

But, wasn't it dangerous? Didn't some of your rockets blow up? Sure, most of them did, because we were pushing the limits of strength of the steel rocket bodies, and took appropriate safety measures. Nobody ever got hurt. Did anybody ever get bitten by the deadly spiders in some of the caves the Student Section explored? No, because we knew that was a possibility, and took appropriate precautions, even without adults to tell us to. Is it possible that something could have gone wrong on one of our adventures? Sure. Could anything have gone wrong on Apollo 11–? Sure, but acceptance of risk is the price of a shot at greatness, and long ago, society was willing to accept some risk in order to allow kids to rise to their maximum potential in science. Today, the only place society seems to accept risk with youngsters is in sports. Quite a change.

A BCRS rocket after its 2,200 foot high voyage. These rockets used a variety of fuels, some rather explosive if not handled correctly.

California Academy of Sciences
Golden Gate Park
San Francisco
March 22, 1950

The Officers of the Academy are pleased to advise that

Mr. Frank Henry Heppner

was elected a

Member

of the California Academy of Sciences on

March 21, 1950

J. Wyatt Durham
Recording Secretary

Chapter 5
OMG!!

In early January of 1975, the *Providence Journal-Bulletin* ran a short article about my bird research. A couple of weeks later, I received a short, informal note from a guy I never heard of, Allen Owen, of Saunderstown, R.I. on "Earth-Air Inc." stationary. The note essentially asked me if I wanted a couple of thousand bucks to do "some project you entertain that might be just a little too wild to put in grant-proposal form." This immediately told me that he knew something about The System, because granting agencies are often staffed by the most risk-aversive people on the planet.

I figured it was a crank letter, but what the hell. So on the 21st of January, I wrote him a two page letter outlining some things I was salivating to do but couldn't afford. Not wanting to push my luck, the total I asked for was about $6,000 (about $25,000 in today's dollars).

About a week later, a small envelope arrived in the Zoology office. It contained a personal check for $14,000 (about $60,000 in today's dollars) made out to me, and a short note from Allen, saying "As the great Nietzsche observed, we can 'overlook a whole cartload of beautiful possibilities in exchange for a sure nothing'." He had given me twice what I'd asked for. Maybe he was the good fairy.

I was stunned. There was no address on the envelope, just a box number. I remember that my first thought was that this was a hell of a mean joke to play on somebody. But there was an account number on the check, so I called my bank, which happened to be the one that was named on the check, and asked if there was enough money in that account to cover the check. After a minute, the teller laughed, and said, "There's PLENTY of money in that account."

Then I realized that he had sent a check made out to me personally. I would have to pay taxes on it, and he wouldn't get a tax deduction. After a complex search, I got his phone number, and explained that it would be better for both of us if he donated the money to the university to get a tax break. He replied that he didn't want the university to take out any overhead (again showing that he knew the system). I told him I'd check it out, and after some negotiation, URI agreed to accept it as a "restricted gift," in which I would do the majority of the bookkeeping. I asked Allen what kind of fiscal reporting he wanted from me, and he replied that he didn't want any; the idea was to free me so I could do my research. How do you like THEM apples?

By the beginning of February, just about a month after the newspaper article appeared, the account was set up and I started spending his money. Today, it takes about 4–6 months to prepare a major grant proposal, about 50% of the money goes for "overhead," and about 20% of an investigator's time is spent filing reports and doing paperwork. Obviously, a much better system than Allen's.

I asked him later if he'd like to visit my lab, just to see what he'd invested in. He was very diffident, "if it was no trouble," etc. Well, he finally came by, and my students and I gave him a show and tell. Turned out he had something to do with buying and selling rare jewels, in which there evidently was money to be made. He was a bit shy, but by his questions, I concluded that he was the brightest guy I'd ever met, and I still hold to that opinion. My students and I were all intimidated, but in a nice way.

His money lasted for three years, and I gave him a final "report" in 1978. It turned out Allen and I had a certain resonance. We both were against the idea of "big science" and thought you could do a lot more if you didn't have the impedimenta of bureaucracy in the way. As I reread the report in preparation for this chapter, I made a discovery that was very gratifying. It turns out that I was thinking as early as 1978 that the solution to how and why birds flew in organized groups lay in mathematics. This turned out to be prophetic, and ahead of its time, as will be discussed later.

I never saw Allen again. I'm thinking he WAS the good fairy.

Chapter 6
Application for Tenure

University faculty have the longest probationary period of any profession. The up-out decision normally comes after 6 years on the job. If the decision is "out," one's academic career is essentially over. In the old days, when academic jobs were far more plentiful than they are today, if it appeared after a couple of years that a candidate wasn't going to make the grade but was reasonably competent, a department would do everything it could to help the unfortunate soul find another job, perhaps at a different kind of college. In my original department—Zoology—at URI we had a guy who was a wonderful teacher, but wasn't, strangely enough for a university professor, terribly interested in research. Before he came anywhere near the critical decision time, URI helped him to get a job at Clemson, an unusual university because it had two separate-but-equal tenure tracks; teaching and research. Turned out to be the best thing possible for him and enabled him to have the last laugh. He became a wildly successful textbook writer and national authority on teaching techniques, and made about twice as much as he would have if he had gotten tenure at URI.

Of course, there was a worm in the apple of this system. If there was somebody a department really wanted to get rid of for whatever reason, it would write wildly enthusiastic letters of reference in the hope that some sucker institution would take him or her off their hands. The same principle applied internally. Got a secretary who is driving everybody crazy? As soon as there's an opening in another department, send off recommendations so warm they had a radioactive glow, and hope that the other department didn't do due diligence.

So, tenure denials were rare. Where they did happen, the outcome was usually tragic for all parties, but they were so unusual that if someone showed early promise, the application for tenure process was almost laughably simple.

I was hired by the Zoology Department in 1969. Having a very good opinion of my own abilities, and a bit of data to back up the opinion, I applied for early promotion and tenure in 1972, about three years ahead of schedule. Below are the contents of my letter to the Chairman of the department requesting early promotion (I've put some explanations in parentheses);

I'd like to more or less go on record as requesting a promotion for next year. In the following I have listed the arguments for and against this proposition.

ARGUMENTS IN FAVOR OF AWARDING PROMOTION TO F. HEPPNER

1. *I deserve it; take a look at my updated CV in my file.*
2. *It won't cost the department anything; with the "raises," I will still be above the minimum for the next higher rank anyway. (*I was already at the top of the salary categories).
3. *I am trustworthy, loyal, helpful, friendly, courteous, kind, cheerful, thrifty, brave, clean, and reverent.* (The Boy Scout Law).
4. *My mother says you should promote me.*
5. *If I am not promoted, a friend of the Family* (Mafia) *in Providence will come down to have a chat with you.*
6. *If I am promoted, the Department will have a thousand years of blissful happiness, and roses will grow through the cracks in the building* (our brand new building had been built by a, unh, *connected* contractor and was falling apart even as the concrete dried).
7. *If I am not promoted, I will flunk all 389 of my students, tell them you told me to, and give them your phone number.*

ARGUMENTS AGAINST AWARDING PROMOTION TO F. HEPPNER

1. *There are no arguments against this promotion.*

Given how serious everyone is about this process today, you will be amused/appalled by the informality. The entire application consisted of the letter, a copy of my resume, copies of my scientific papers and the names of three outside referees. Six pages besides the reprints. When I became chairman of the Biological Sciences Department in the '00s for a couple of years, I handled three promotion/tenure requests. Their average length was over 300 pages. How come so much paper? Part of the reason had to do with a rare tenure denial case that occurred in the Zoology Department in the '70s that ruined the career not only of the person who was denied, but the chairman of the department at the time. This case is discussed elsewhere. These lessons were not lost among administrators, and ever after chairs, deans, and presidents made sure there would always be enough documentation to ensure that an appeal for a denial of tenure would be fruitless. The amount of time wasted by all parties in this endeavor has been staggering. This follows the military principle called CYA (Cover Your Ass).

Oh, by the way, my application was approved. Thus emboldened, I applied for promotion to full professor a few years later, and in 1979 I was the youngest full at URI.

Chapter 7
How Bureaucratic Constipation
Starts in Colleges

I've elsewhere alluded to a disputed tenure case that I believe had a significant effect on the way URI goes about its business today. The story had a sad ending, and some of the people involved are still around, so I'll change some names and circumstances. It was always known as "The Hawker Case," after the center of the controversy, Dr. Stephen L. Hawker. I didn't find any reference to it in my own files, and it has been lost in institutional memory to all but the oldest of old-timers, but I thought it was sufficiently important to poke around in the URI university archives (thanks to Sarina Rodrigues), and there I found 13 *boxes* of papers having to do with the case, which stretched from 1968–1974. That must be some kind of record.

Hawker came to the Department of Zoology at URI in the mid 1960s, and in 1968 was informed that his contract wouldn't be renewed in 1969. This seems early for the mandatory tenure decision. The reasons offered by the Department of Zoology for the non-renewal seemed vague by today's terms, but had to do more with teaching than research, which was highly unusual for the times. If your research was good and got good journal press, you could give your large-class lectures in Swahili, while naked and drunk, and nobody would care. I'm reconstructing here, but this was the period when the department was expanding and ambitious, and the other members of the department may have felt that his research was too old-fashioned. Whatever the reason, the non-renewal vote was unanimous. I should point out that at the time, untenured faculty had very few "rights."

Hawker immediately started the first of the many appeals that were open to him. He was vocal in anti-Vietnam war circles, and immediately had allies who claimed that he was being persecuted for his anti-war views. I came on the scene in 1969 and the department seemed decidedly non-political, so I never really bought that scenario. That he might have had some personal run-ins with a couple of the senior faculty who were on the conservative side is entirely possible.

I still don't know exactly how I came to fit in this picture. There's nothing that I could later find in the records, and I quickly discovered at the time that it was a no-no in casual conversation. What follows is what I assembled from memory (and the archives) much later.

At about the time of Hawker's first rejection, the Zoology Department hired a very distinguished University of Michigan geneticist named Samuel Taylor out of retirement to take over Hawker's intro course, Bio 2, the huge non-major's course that later I was assigned to. This was extremely unusual for the time—why on earth would Taylor leave Michigan and come to URI?—and I can only conclude that there was some personal connection between Taylor and Rhode Island. I'm guessing that he directly replaced Hawker, but I found no record that would support that idea, logical as it seems. Taylor was a delightful elderly gentleman in his '70s, and I heard a number of stories about how students in Bio 2 took advantage of him, mercifully without his knowledge. As an example, when he gave an exam, he would collect all the answer sheets AND the question sheets. Then, the following semester he would give exactly the same questions on exams. This was like manna from heaven for the Greek system and the dorms, whose members would memorize and share the answers to the previous semester's questions. When I started his old course in 1969, naturally I changed the questions. There were screams of outrage and unfairness from the students who had wasted all that time memorizing Taylor's questions and answers.

The announcement for the job I applied for appeared in March of 1969, to start in Fall 1969. It was very odd for such an opening to appear that late in the academic year, but my tentative conclusion is that Taylor was beginning to show signs of being unable to teach the course any more. The department didn't really want to put Hawker back on the job in late '68, but by March 1969, no alternative had appeared, and they had to put a body in front of the class by fall. Today, a department would simply hire any one of the dozens of jobless Ph.D.'s hanging around universities, but this was unknown at the time. Somehow, the department got permission to advertise a tenure track job (Hawker's) while Hawker was still on the scene. That was what I walked into as a greenhorn in Fall of 1969.

Nobody in the department talked about the case, so what I learned about it came from the grapevine and the student newspaper, where Hawker had become a Hero of the People. At the end of his first round of appeals, which were rejected, he had been put into a no-show job for a year, and the expectation was that he would look for another job during that time.

Unfortunately, what would have been relatively easy for him when he was first bounced became impossible, because now he was officially a "troublemaker."

I tried to keep my distance from the whole thing, but I have to admit that I did wonder a bit what would happen to MY job, if Hawker got HIS job back. He had an office in another part of campus, so I hardly ever ran into him, but one time we were in the same place at the same time, and I asked him about something that puzzled me. His advocates were publicly savaging the Zoology Department and its senior members, while Hawker was saying all he wanted to do was have this all settled and go back to teaching his classes and rejoin the department, which he loved. So, I asked him why, if the department was so terrible, he was fighting so hard to stay here? He replied that if he lost his appeals he'd never get another academic job again, but if he won, he'd be able to claim persecution, and would be able to get a job on another campus which favored his political persuasion. I knew he had both a good point and a family, so I didn't repeat the story—he seemed like a nice enough guy, and he WAS a field biologist, so we belonged to the same fraternity. Besides, I had already gotten tenure by the time his case was finally resolved, so I was "safe" no matter what happened to him.

Ultimately, Hawker's appeals depended not on the facts of the case, but on whether he had received due process. None of the appeals bodies concluded that there had been a violation of due process, but in those days, there tended not to BE a due process, in a formal sense. The department did handle things poorly in a procedural way, and this lesson was not lost on subsequent generations of administrators.

Hawker lost his last appeal in 1974, and by this time, everybody, including his advocates, was just getting tired. Besides, the campus had new things to worry about, like the first energy crisis. Hawker left campus and more-or-less disappeared. However, the Zoology Department was left in a shambles after his departure. The senior members Hawker had complained about, and who were vilified in the student paper, turned in their mobility coupons, and went to other, better jobs. The chairman quit, and a few years later left academia. The department, which had been a rising star, now was identified as a nest of right-wing asps, and got last place at the feeding trough of campus resources, many of which were administered by the progressive Faculty Senate, which had been one of Hawker's allies.

Perhaps the most long-lasting effect was that administrators, from the president on down, looked at the staggering amounts of time they had been forced to spend on the issue, and decided that prevention was the best medicine. From then on, there was a procedure and a form for everything. Never again would somebody try an appeal of anything on the basis of lack of due process, or inadequate documentation. The cost to the university in time spent on excess ass-covering, and hiring extra administrative personnel to handle all the paperwork has been enormous, and I venture to guess that today, nobody really knows why college administrative procedures on almost anything reflect an excess of circumspection. The Hawker Case established an administrative culture of caution that persists today, in matters great and small. This provided an almost perfect example of the genesis of what has been described as "bureaucratic constipation."

This is the kind of story I hate to tell, because there were no heroes and no winners. Hawker vanished, and I heard later that he had died of a heart attack in 1987. The ex-department chair's story is a little happier—sort of. After leaving URI he bought a nursery in Vermont, and I remained more or less in contact over the years. For him to have to leave was a tragedy, because he was a good teacher and researcher. He retired to Florida and passed away in 2017.

Chapter 8
Multi-Media

Professional teaching and educational theory are very faddish. In higher education we have gone through Audio-Visual, "Keller Plan," Personalized System of Instruction, Programmed Learning, Connectivism, Multimedia, The Perry Method, and the latest, "Blended Learning." Most of these ideas were introduced with great fanfare, little evidence, and limitless commercial possibilities for folks like Steve and Bill. They are often started by charismatic gurus who know how to attract public and press attention, hence Keller Plan, and Perry Method. They last until the next wizard comes along. Now we have to have one child-one computer in the public schools. And as we all know, American educational performance has gone up in direct proportion to children's access to technology.

"Multimedia" in education now means using images, sound, and text in a single presentation on a computer screen. In the 1970s, it meant using more than one slide projector at a time. During my teaching career, I was always an enthusiast and promoter for the latest and best technology in teaching, because I was a gadget freak at heart, and loved anything having to do with photography. My crowning glory was the last lecture in Bio 2 in URI's Edwards Auditorium, which used six Carousel projectors and 960 slides, all set to music, and manually changed. Took weeks of rehearsal. Alas, much like the first bloom of love, new techniques in teaching qualities that were first charming and quirky turn out to be nasty and annoying.

In 1972, the Zoology Department had a new building, the Biological Sciences Center, more commonly known as (and pronounced like) BISC. It was a controversial building in many ways, but in the original budget, there was no provision for any kind of projection facility in the auditorium.

In that year I wrote letters to the Zoology Chair, the Audio-Visual Director, and the Academic VP, shamelessly promoting the idea that the auditorium should have the latest and best audiovisual equipment so we could do Multimedia in grand style. This was the same year I was applying for tenure, so there was a bonus in that I could portray myself as forward-thinking, if a bit cocky.

In truth, when the dust settled there really WAS an advantage to early multimedia under certain circumstances. If you were trying to compare

35

something, say before-and-after, like a plant before and after it was infected with a disease, you had a much better idea of what was going on if you saw the before and after pictures side-by-side rather than one after the other, as you would with a single projector. Of course, you could produce exactly the same effect by having both images on the same projector slide and using a really big screen, but before Photoshop it was a pain in the butt to make such slides.

The powers that be were sufficiently impressed by the pitch to give me the go-ahead to prepare a grant proposal to the RI Champlin Foundations, which was duly approved in mid-decade. It was for a staggering amount of money for the time, $122,000, and for about a year I was as happy as a guy with hives in a backscratcher factory, because I got to play with all the gadgets. In the mid-1990s I got another grant from the same source to upgrade the facility.

In retrospect, very few instructors took up the multimedia challenge, even after first-class equipment was available. The fact was, it took a tremendous amount of time to make these presentations, and the handwriting was on the wall by the early '80s that faculty were going to be judged primarily by their prowess at grant getting, and as long as there weren't armed protests from their undergraduate students, it didn't matter much what happened in their big classes. Today, with increasing attention given to retaining students and their tuition, the pendulum may be swinging the other way.

There is no question, however, that students enjoyed these presentations more than most straight lectures. Whether this translated into more learning I was never able to establish. I suspect the same is true today, where the almost universal method of presentation in large classes has been a series of Powerpoint slides, the majority of which are incredibly boring, because they're just text outlines. So I really don't know which is worse; the old-fashioned straight lecturer of my early days, whose monotone could be used by the Bureau of Standards, or the contemporary lecturer who presents an endless series of Powerpoint slides while talking to the screen with his or her back to the class. *Plus* ça *change, plus c'est la même chose.*

Chapterlet 3 • College 1

During my years of teaching huge freshman classes at URI, I had a great deal of sympathy with students who weren't doing very well. This may have been because at the end of my first semester at Rensselaer Polytechnic Institute in Troy, New York in 1958, I was as mathematically close as possible to flunking out without actually doing so. I had a 1.8 average. But why RPI, when I grew up 12 miles away from Berkeley to which I was also admitted?

I think it was because I was born with a sense of wanderlust, which I was fortunately able to exercise during my career. One of my recent books was called "The Seventy Year Train Ride; 500,000 Miles by Rail." I loved my parents, and loved the Bay Area, but I wanted to go as far away from home as possible. Before jet travel, New York was as distant as the moon as far as I was concerned.

Going away to college was another thing that has changed mightily since then and has affected how one teaches first-year students. I still have the home movies I took when I departed. My parents took me to the Oakland train station on a September day, along with two of my best friends. I was 17 years old, all my worldly possessions were in two small suitcases, and I was about to climb aboard the Southern Pacific Railroad's *San Francisco Overland* train for a five-day, 3,000 mile trip to Troy. Going away by yourself to college was essentially the transition from kid to adult.

Leaving for college in 1958, and becoming (more or less) an adult at the same time.

When I was a professor at URI, one of my favorite activities was to go down to the freshman dorms when the frosh were checking in for the first time around Labor Day. When I started, in 1969, it was mostly students I chatted with, but this changed over the years as the students began to bring more *stuff* with them. Electronic equipment. Sports equipment. A Saks Fifth Avenue store's worth of clothes for the girls. Eventually it required a rental trailer to hold all this stuff, pulled by the parents' car. Even without the gear, as time passed it became increasingly rare to see a kid come to college by himself/herself. Even if a freshman lived in Westerly, 20 miles away, Mom and Dad would trundle the offspring off for first day of college.

How come? Well, I'd have to be a sociologist to venture an informed opinion, but lack of that credential never slowed me down. For many years, as it became the norm for parents to protect kids to the point of suffocation, when they became college students many of them floundered with their newfound independence and needed parental assistance for the transition.

From my arrival at RPI in '58, to my graduation in '62 after I transferred to Berkeley at the end of my first year, I had about 40 college teachers. Did they have any effect on me? The vast majority of them reside in my memory like the fog drifting in over the Golden Gate Bridge. Two of them changed my life for the better. They were as different as one could imagine. One of the reasons I decided to write this book was to show present and future college teachers that they can have an enormous positive impact on their students and the larger society should they choose to, and devote the time and effort needed to produce that end.

My first hero was named Robert Stebbins, and I remember him because he showed me what it was like to LOVE the field you were in. Bob (we later became academically close enough that I would dare to use his first name) was not remarkable in the formalities of college teaching. He was a herpetologist (a student of reptiles and amphibians). His lectures were ordinary; not bad but not memorable either. It was in the lab that he shined. One day we were talking about the life histories of rattlesnakes. He told us that one kind, the sidewinder, had an unusual way of moving across sand dunes. There were about 15 of us in the class, and he told us to gather around an open area in the lab. He poured a bucket of sand on the floor, then emptied the contents of a bag he had been carrying on to the sand. The little sidewinder rattlesnake that had been inside the bag gathered himself, then slowly undulated over the sand exactly as Bob had said he would. We had all jumped back when the snake appeared, but Bob said, "No, No. They know when you mean them no harm." When the snake reached the edge of the sand, Bob gently reached down, and picked up the snake with two hands, one behind its head, the other supporting the body. He then placed the snake inside an open terrarium. We all let go our breath, which we had been holding.

I was at the time, at the peak of my Cynical Undergraduate period, and thought to myself that the snake was defanged. What kind of idiot would willingly pick up a deadly snake? After the snake was in the cage, Bob said that he would demonstrate how this species fed. He reached into a cage, pulled out a mouse, and dropped it in with the snake. Boom! Dead mouse. That instantly turned me into a Stebbins fan.

Back in the day, there was enough money in college budgets to allow long field trips for biology classes. We went on a week-long field trip with Bob to the Mojave Desert. Deserts were like heaven for herpetologists. We used three university cars, and I rode next to Bob, who drove the first car. All through the hundreds of miles of the Central Valley, Bob drove like a granny, exactly on the speed limit, hands clutched tightly to the wheel. Then we began the long climb up Tehachapi Pass. After we cleared the summit and the road flattened out, we started to speed up. Then sped up a little more. Then I glanced over at the speedometer, and said, "Unh, Dr. Stebbins, we're going 95 miles an hour." He gave an embarrassed laugh, backed off the gas, and said, "Sorry, that always happens when I can smell the desert." Three more days in the Mojave with Stebbins showed me what it was like to be passionate about what you studied, and I resolved to find something like that myself. And I did.

From Bob Stebbins I learned about loving a field. From Richard Eakin, I learned what a powerful effect a big lecturer could have on students. Eakin was a well-known and respected researcher at Berkeley, with over 200 publications, but he somehow found the time and energy to be one of the most outstanding teachers at Berkeley, winning every teaching award and a Guggenheim Fellowship

He taught two big courses, General Zoology and an upper division Embryology course. I was one of the 200-some students in that course. Oh,

I forgot to mention that he was also an artist and made all the drawings for his courses on the auditorium blackboard. Students didn't schedule themselves any classes in the hour before, so they could come in early to copy his drawings in those days before overhead projectors.

Eakin emphasized that scientists needed to be precise, and he demonstrated that by ALWAYS starting lecture at 10:00:00 and ending EXACTLY at 10:50:00 with the last word. Much later I got to know Eakin, and I found out how he did it. He wrote each lecture out word for word, changing and editing them like a play. He timed and revised them until they were exactly 50 minutes long (a 50 minute lecture is 28 double-spaced typed pages) then memorized them. But he had the astounding ability to edit in his head, so if a student asked a question, he would juggle things around in his brain as he was talking so he could still end exactly on time.

I should mention here that it was always Eakin's custom, when the lecture started to say "Good morning." It was like that was the point where you started your stopwatch.

It was the tradition at the time at Berkeley that the last lecture of the semester be the best quality the professor could give, and should contain some sort of lesson or message that would pull the course together and try to make sense of everything. When Eakin's last lecture came, the auditorium was filled not only with current students, but the aisles were packed with former students, and TA's from many departments.

One thing was different right away. He didn't say, "Good morning," like usual. The theme of the lecture was his good fortune to have been able to spend his life in science. He had been lucky enough to be a graduate student in the lab of a Nobel Prize winner named Spemann, He described both the joy and the hard work involved, and the huge personal rewards that came with the possibility of making new scientific discoveries.

As he talked, I became inflamed. I decided that when I finished up my education, *I wanted to be just like him!* It's up to others to judge how successful I've been, but my whole career in science was inspired by that man and that class.

At last, he came to the end of the lecture. How could he possibly wrap this up? He finally said, "It is my parting wish that you will have a life as rich and rewarding as mine has been." He paused, and slowly looked out over the class, maybe a touch sadly. Finally, he said *"Good morning*–and goodbye." The lights instantly went out, and when they slowly came up, he was gone.

How's that for a smash ending? Sixty years ago, and I remember it like it was yesterday. Somehow, I don't think Powerpoints are going to be able to provide the same experience.

And that is one of the takehomes I'd like to leave. If you're a professor, out in your classes somewhere there is a kid whose life you can literally make better, even if you never meet him or her. That's one of the hidden rewards of being a college teacher.

Chapter 9
The Instructional Development Program

When I came to URI in 1969 there was a curious belief and practice about the preparation someone needed to teach college courses. By law, to teach biology to an 18-year-old high school kid in the 12th grade, a prospective high school teacher must have had 18 credits of professional education courses, a semester of observation of a class taught by a master teacher in the discipline, then a semester of supervised teaching, before they obtained a teaching certificate. However, it appears that after that same 18-year-old kid graduated from high school, a miracle happened. In the three months between high school graduation and entry to college, that kid's brain *matured so much over the summer* that his college freshman biology teacher needed only a pleasant smile and some knowledge of the subject to be considered a competent, professional teacher. And then people scratched their heads and wondered why kids who had done well in high school then bombed as college freshmen.

In glancing recently at a Google question, "do professors need to take education courses to teach?" it appears that nothing has changed very much. Then, as now, most of academia requires no professional training or supervised practice in teaching to become a college professor. After scratching one's head, one realizes that custom and practice means either that, A) High school teachers don't really need professional training, or B) College teachers do. I argue that B) is correct.

In the '70s, there was a nascent movement that suggested that college teachers really *could* benefit from some exposure to educational psychology, teaching techniques, educational theory, etc., and it might not be a bad idea to throw in a little supervised teaching. Academia may be politically liberal, but it is operationally extremely conservative, and this idea was not greeted warmly in all quarters and was actively resisted in others. Despite this, "Teaching and Learning" centers began to appear on campuses around the US, typically squirreled away in a basement someplace and living on a shoestring.

Surprisingly, URI was a pioneer in this area, and in the '70s, the Instructional Development Program (IDP) was started up by Glenn and Bette Erickson, who were trained in one of the first programs of its kind at University of Wisconsin.

In the late '70s, the Ericksons obtained a grant from the Lilly Foundation to set up a Teaching Fellows program at URI. Basically, for a year selected faculty members met once a week at the faculty center (now closed), the Ericksons gave a presentation, and the participants got a free dinner. Periodically, one of the Ericksons would come to your class to see how you were doing. I was one of the first 20 or so Teaching Fellows.

It changed my life. Suddenly, I learned what it meant to be a *professional* teacher, whether in college or before. You had to learn about developmental psychology. You had to know the theory of testing and measurement. You had to learn about organizing classes. You had to practice public speaking. All of a sudden, the indifferentness I had seen in my students suddenly made sense, and even more importantly, I learned that *now I could change things for the better*. It was BS that all you had to know was your subject to be an effective college teacher. You had to know teaching techniques. Sure, there were exceptional, rare, outstanding teachers who had never been trained formally, but they got that way intuitively. Einstein didn't have to be taught relativity. Newton didn't have to be taught the laws of motion. Everybody else has to have some instruction.

I was on fire about all this stuff. This was going to revolutionize college teaching. Then in 1981 a bomb dropped. The Academic Vice President announced that he was going to discontinue the program in 1982 for economic reasons. The former IDP faculty fellows flooded the VP's office with letters.

I am delighted to report a happy ending to this story. Somehow, the money was found to rescue the program, and it continues today, living from hand to mouth—but living. Thousands of URI faculty and teaching assistants, and the university itself, have benefited from it.

Chapter 10
Peer Evaluation and Confidentiality

The '70s were a time of profound and upsetting changes at URI. The school itself was evolving from a sleepy regional aggie school to a research university, financial support from the state was starting to erode while enrollments increased, the faculty union added one more layer of complexity to university governance, and the Student Movement, which had been slow to come to URI, was beginning to make its presence felt in a significant way.

While all this was happening, there was a sea change in how the university regarded confidentiality. It would have a far-reaching effect on how faculty looked at themselves, and their professional relationship to their colleagues and students.

The proximate event was the institution of the concept of peer review in faculty evaluations. This was primarily a result of unionization, and the union's apparent desire to erode the power of university administration. Whether this power needed eroding is a separate matter, but it was clear to everyone in the faculty, whatever their political position, that a power struggle was developing between the two entities.

Making the issue sharper was an erosion in the sense that evaluations, whether of colleagues or students, were to be regarded as privileged and confidential. For the first time, faculty had to be concerned about the legal, and possibly extra-campus implications of their actions and judgments in written evaluations of colleagues and students. This was something new for the professorate.

Prior to the mid-'70s, letters of recommendation, for either students' grad/med school applications or faculty promotion/tenure were considered absolutely privileged. If you had negative information about a candidate, and could back it up, you could feel free to make those negative comments without fear of later repercussions to yourself. However, a series of lawsuits against individual faculty members who had negative comments in students' letters of recommendation for grad or medical school made faculty wary about making negative comments, even if they were based in fact. The amount of time spent by the faculty involved in defending these suits was staggering, even if in the event the suit was not successful.

There was no simple resolution to this issue, and there are repercussions even today. For example, you dare not directly say anything negative in a letter of recommendation. Faculty have been sued because candidates didn't get into medical school as the result of a bad recommendation. So, suppose you really feel conscience bound to tell a school or employer that they are taking a risk by picking up this person? A code has developed, at least for student recommendations.

A very short letter of recommendation; shorter than you would expect given the amount of contact you had with the student, says "red flag." It is an unspecific warning, but at least it can't come back to bite you, and does give a heads-up to the recipient of the letter. For this reason, many of us who teach students who get a good grade in our giant course, but who we don't really know because the course is so big, advise students who ask us for letters not to use us as references, because our letter is going to be necessarily short, and might be taken as a red flag letter.

The other area of concern was student cheating. One of the products of the student movement was the establishment of an elaborate judicial system by which a student could defend him/herself against an accusation of cheating. Almost overnight, we went from, "He's looking on his neighbor's paper! Flunk him," to a system where the evidentiary standards for failing a student for cheating had to approach that required in capital murder cases. A couple of the cases I had in this category were actually pretty funny.

In one, after the final was corrected, but before the grades were submitted, two members of the basketball team (I am presuming) broke into the office of my lab coordinator over a weekend, broke into her desk, obtained the grade book, and changed both of their grades (but no others) from "F" to "A", using a different color ink to make the change. As soon as I made the discovery, I filed the papers to have them dismissed from the university. There was a hearing, and my petition was denied because I didn't have any physical evidence that THEY had made the change. I was permitted to allow their "F's" to stand, because I was able to argue successfully that whoever had changed their letter grade, it wasn't me.

Another one was even more bizarre. Students were told to bring their student ID cards to the final exam, and that we would spot check them. We waited until the students settled down, then the TA's went around the room, and asked students at random to show their cards. Everything went well until they came to one guy who became tremendously flustered at the request, then bolted out of his seat and ran from the room. Alas, he had forgotten to take the exam with him, and he had already filled in the name of the student for whom he was acting as amanuensis.

I duly asked that the student be dismissed from the university for cheating, and he appealed. There followed a hearing where he gave his version, which follows.

He readily admitted that he hadn't taken the exam, but in no way did he engage someone to take the exam for him. He was from Pawtucket, and it seems that at the beginning of finals week he had been playing baseball at home and had hurt his arm badly enough that he couldn't write. So he decided to stay home to recover (without calling any of his professors to request an incomplete, of course).

At the same time, his campus roommate had a visiting guest. The accused phoned his roommate on the day of the exam, with the intention of asking the roommate to contact me to explain the situation (he didn't state why he had to use his roommate as an intermediary). However, his roommate was out when he called, and the guest took the call. The guest was *so sorry* for the student, didn't know how to contact me, and the exam was only about an hour away, so he decided to take the exam *for* the student, as a gesture of friendliness. He panicked when he was asked for an ID, because the injured student hadn't told him about the requirement to bring it to the exam.

Breathtaking, isn't it? But the student movement was so powerful, that in the new cheating review procedure, I wasn't allowed to cross-examine the student. Ultimately, the student won his case because I couldn't *prove* that he had engaged somebody to take the exam. I was allowed to fail him, however, because without the final, he didn't have enough points to pass.

Unfortunately, prosecuting these cases took a staggering amount of time (alluded to in a letter I found to the Dean of Students), so the whole emphasis in giving important exams shifted from catching cheaters to preventing cheating. For example, using multiple forms of the exam, and making sure that students sitting next to each other didn't have the same form of the exam, or printing the exam with small type, making it more difficult to eavesdrop. These tricks were effective, but almost all of them added time to the task of administering exams.

Chapterlet 4 · College 2

When I left Rensselaer after my first year, my gradepoint was 2.0. When I graduated from Berkeley, it was 2.8, yet I was admitted to grad school in Zoology at San Francisco State University. The fact that I scored a 98% on the GRE's probably didn't hurt. Years later, after I became a professor, and was trying to advise undergrads with erratic records like mine, I took a new look at my own record to see if I could figure out why it was so bouncy.

At Berkeley, if I liked the subject and the professor, I got an A. If I was indifferent to either, I got a C. I always had broad interests and was a voracious reader, not limiting myself to scientific topics, but time is always important to an undergraduate, and when time was limited, interest in a course often took priority over getting a good grade. That was certainly my case. It may be different today.

Perfect lecturing techniques were not absolutely required for faculty memorability at Berkeley. I took one course in the new field of molecular biology that had absolutely no interest for me before I took it as a requirement. That course was taught by the distinguished scientist Daniel Mazia. He was a good lecturer, and a genuinely nice man as I discovered, but he had the largest single collection of annoying lecture mannerisms I ever encountered. He lectured in a large hall with a chemistry bench in front. He would begin at the stage right side of the bench, mark an "X" on the top with his chalk, and then turn and face the blackboard, a head position that didn't vary during the whole lecture. He would then start writing with his right hand, and erasing with his left, so that when he reached the stage left side, the board would be clean. He would then walk back to his original position, erase the "X" with his thumb, then write a new one and begin again.

But that wasn't the worst part. He had this—thing—where spit would gather in the corner of his mouth, and then fly off in random directions. After about a week, nobody sat in the first row. After a while, those in the first 10 rows or so would spontaneously wipe their mouths with their sleeves every now and then. Nobody said anything about it or complained. Eccentricity was not just tolerated; it was encouraged. He was such a good lecturer that people were willing to forgive his little—peculiarities, and he helped me to understand the molecular stuff that I couldn't avoid in my later career.

In my senior year, I took an ornithology course with a famous bird scientist named Alden Miller. I was the only undergrad among 10 students.

Miller was an okay lecturer but put him in the field and he was an inspiration. I don't know how old he was, late '60s maybe, but when he ran up a hill after some damn bird on the Hastings wildlife reservation in Carmel, California all you could see was his white hair as he led the pack of gasping grad students behind.

One day, after class, he asked me to stay for a couple of minutes. It seems he had some kind of grant that called for him to hire undergrad students to work part time in the Museum of Vertebrate Zoology (MVZ). I was the only undergrad he knew at the moment, so would I like the job? It only paid $1.50/hour, he said. $1.50/hour? That was a FORTUNE! At the time I was working a 12-hour shift on Saturdays hauling 50 pound bags of flour in a bakery for $0.75/an hour. It took me about 3 milliseconds to say "yes!"

Perhaps I should have asked him what the job entailed before I took it.

The Job

After I accepted the position, Miller took me over to the museum to introduce me to my new boss, Dr. Frank Pitelka, and my immediate supervisor, a grad student whose name I disremember. Pitelka, like most of the MVZ faculty was known for his field work, and as a result was pretty rugged and salty. He was a spiffy dresser however, and usually wore a bow tie and vest, which matched his white beard nicely.

Miller introduced me, and Pitelka gave me a few welcoming words in his basso profundo voice, then I was escorted out and didn't see him for weeks. The grad student who was responsible for training me then took over, and started to explain my jobs, which were two in number (in addition to running errands and being a general dogsbody).

First, I learned that the MVZ had thousands, or maybe tens of thousands of disarticulated bird skeletons (there were hundreds of thousands of specimens in total) contained in special acid-free cardboard boxes. Every specimen had a unique serial number, and the way it was explained to me, the MVZ was worried that in a severe earthquake, some of the boxes might open, and the bones from different skeletons might be mixed. I wasn't told till later WHY any of this museum stuff was important, but it was made VERY clear to me that this possible mixing had to be avoided at any cost, possibly lives were at stake, and that was where I came in. It seemed that every bone in the box had to be marked with a 6-digit serial number so that if there were a spill and mix, the bones could be restored to their original box. This sort of made sense to me, and then my "guide" took me over to a workbench where I would do my work.

There was a very powerful lamp mounted to the desk, along with a strong, large magnifying glass on a movable stand. I would do the lettering with a needle-point quill pen, and use Higgens Eternal Ink. He then brought over a cart that had several drawer/trays slipped into it. Each tray had several dozen very small boxes. My guy picked up one of the boxes and explained that each box contained an entire bird skeleton's worth of single bones, and my job was to letter the six-digit ID number on each of the bones. Including the toes. I asked what kind of bird the box contained. He said, "sparrow," and spilled the contents out on the desk. I didn't use strong language in those days, but today, I would have said, "You gotta be s—in' me!" But then, it WAS $1.50/hour.

My other main task was far more interesting, and today, I'm rather surprised that they entrusted it to me. I guess they assumed that if I took an ornithology course, I must be interested in birds, but that wasn't correct. I was a reptile guy due to youthful activities and birds, meh, I had no interest.

So I was singularly unprepared for my job. The MVZ was at that time sending collecting expeditions all over the world, and the ornithologists would collect and put up the bird skins in the field. They would attach cardboard tags to the legs that would contain date and exact location data. My recollection is that they didn't put any species identifications, even in pencil, on the tags. My guess at the time was that they felt that a proper ID could only be made by comparing the specimen to other museum specimens, and I supposed that they didn't want to bias the people back in the museum, but I was never sure.

At any rate, my job was to carefully unpack the incoming crates, put the specimens in museum trays, and then make a tentative ID of each specimen to a family category, assemble them together with similar specimens, then pass them on to the appropriate ornithologist for final identification.

This was almost overwhelming at first, because other than what I saw in ornithology course, I could barely tell a sparrow from a seagull. However, when you're 20, not only do you have no brains, you have no fear either, so the fact that I was totally unqualified to do this only provided a few milliseconds of hesitation.

I had been advised not to bother the scientists or the grad students if I was stumped unless I had used all the resources available to me first. These were not inconsiderable. I was allowed to open the museum cases to check out my guess to an actual identified specimen, but there was one case (or maybe two) that I was instructed NEVER, EVER to open in the course of my routine duties.

That was the case that contained the "type specimens." It was explained that type specimens were distributed all over the world, and were the physical specimens that defined the characteristics of a species, just like the platinum-iridium "Standard Metre" bar in Paris defined the length of the meter. These type specimens were used to define whether a species was endangered.

To emphasize the importance of these treasures, I was instructed that in case of fire or other natural disaster, I was to attempt to rescue these type specimens, even at risk of my life, if there were no officials around to do it. I started to take my job a lot more seriously after that.

I'd usually begin the ID process by starting with the Peterson Field Guide to the Birds that we used in class. This was helpful, and usually definitive for US birds, but we had specimens coming in from all over the world, although primarily from North and South America.

There were copies of two enormous multivolume reference tomes that I could also use; Peters and Ridgway. I had to learn a staggering amount of anatomical vocabulary just to dip my toes in. Pretty heady stuff for a biology undergraduate.

After a couple of weeks, I started to get the hang of it, and after a while, it would become a fun game. I'd key out, or otherwise identify a specimen, then go to the cases to see if I got it or came close. My batting average got pretty good, but then I had one specimen, I think it may have been from Alaska, that had me stumped. It looked sort of familiar, but whatever it was, I just couldn't nail it.

I was starting to fall behind, when I saw that Director Pitelka's door was open, which usually meant that he was amenable to visitors. I went up and knocked on his door. He told me to enter, and I sidled in, tugged at my forelock, and said, "Dr. Pitelka, I'm Frank, I'm one of the museum apprentices, and I've been trying to identify this specimen for almost three hours." I held it out in my palm. "I've tried to key it out, and I don't know how many cases I've looked in, but I'm stumped, and I'd be very grateful if you could maybe give me a clue."

He looked at the bird, then he looked up at me with an expression of amazement, then he looked at the bird again.

"What did you say your name was?

"Unh, Frank, Sir."

"And you've been working here for how many months?"

"About three, Sir."

"And you really don't know what this bird is, after all that?"

"Unh, yessir, I really don't"

He looked at the bird again, then looked up at me as if he were viewing some strange species of insect for the first time.

"That, young man, is a Chickadee."

The instant he said it, I recognized what it was, and was dumbfounded that I had somehow missed it. I was convinced that any possible career I might have in the sciences was now over. I clutched the ruin-bringing specimen in my hand, tried not to faint, and backed out the door, proclaiming my thanks and apologies for bothering him.

Once I was downstairs, and contemplating whether leaping off the Golden Gate Bridge, or letting one of the rattlesnakes in the reptile lab bite me would be better, I heard a roar of laughter from Pitelka's office. Nobody ever mentioned it to me for the rest of my stay at the MVZ, but many years later, when I was a biologist and saw Pitelka at a meeting, he asked me if I'd identified any good Chickadees lately.

Chapter 11
A Matter of Survival

Colleges are institutions that of their nature reflect changes in society. My alma mater, Berkeley, listed majors in Irrigation, and Railroad Engineering in its 1901 catalog. At URI, between the 1998–1999 catalog and the 2018–2019 catalog, 14 majors were either added or deleted. As society changes, it is natural that colleges and universities evolve to recognize those evolutions. For those who work in those colleges, however, change may not always be so welcome.

Since the middle of the nineteenth century, when universities began to split up their department of Natural Philosophy into subdisciplines, there have traditionally been Botany (plants) and Zoology (animals) departments, rather than Biology departments containing both specialties. Until the mid-twentieth century, Botany and Zoology pretty much existed as separate but equal entities, and that was the structure at URI.

However, starting in the '50s, with Disney's "True-Life Adventures" in the movies, and the '60s "Wild Kingdom" on TV, Zoology began to come into the ascendancy. Why, an undergraduate Zoology major could—study lions in Africa! Tag sharks in Fiji! Free Willy! And an undergraduate Botany major could—? Given the macho nature of many of the things Zoology majors began to aspire to, Botany began to have a bit of a fey image. This was both wildly unfair and inaccurate. Many of the great, and most rugged explorers in history were botanists. The then-current botanists at URI worked in the deserts under a roasting sun, or in the tropics dodging tse-tse flies. Nevertheless, the PR machine said that Zoology was cool and Botany was scholarly, and that was the kiss of death for enrollments.

Also, as requirements for admission to medical school became more formalized, students discovered that many of the required courses for med school could be counted toward the major in Zoology, but were extra electives in Botany, thus increasing the number of courses pre-meds majoring in Botany had to take.

The result was that by the '70s, enrollments in Zoology were disproportionately increasing, while enrollments in Botany were decreasing. This was about the time that, as state financial support for URI decreased, the importance of undergraduate tuition increased. A department that could not recruit large numbers of tuition-paying undergraduates was looking at the blindfold and the last cigarette.

The largest source of enrollments (and recruiting opportunities) lay in the introductory courses. In my association with URI, there had always been two intro biology "tracks;" one for majors and their allies, and the other for general education. In the '60s and '70s, with university gen-ed specific course requirements, the non-major's courses, Biology 101(Botany) and Biology 102 (Zoology) were huge. The majors' courses, Botany 111 and Zoology 111 were big, but not elephantine.

There was an anomaly in the Bio 101–102 sequence, and I noticed it right away when I began teaching. To satisfy general education requirements, a student had to take both courses, but it was set up so that a student could take EITHER the Botany course or the Zoology course first. This made no sense because, if you were teaching (say) the Zoology course in the fall semester, most of your students would not have had a college biology course, but a substantial minority would—those who had been on campus the previous semester. In the spring semester if you taught the Botany part, most of your students would already have had an introduction to genetics, but many wouldn't. The result was that about a third of your course was a repetition of the biology (genetics, etc.) that a big chunk of your students had already been exposed to. So much of your course was a repetition.

I found out that it was the Botany department that insisted on this structure, and it had nothing to do with pedagogy. In a letter from the Zoology Chair to the Botany Chair in 1972, he outlined the problem, and proposed a solution. What he suggested is that one course be made a PREREQUISITE to the other. So a student would have to start with one course, and move to the next the following semester. If he couldn't get into the beginning course of the sequence in fall because it was full, he could begin next semester.

So what's the matter with this? There was a significant number of students who either dropped out of school, or switched to a technical major where they didn't have to take non-major biology, between first and second semesters. So, if your department teaches the second semester course of a two-course sequence, you will have fewer enrollments than the department that teaches the first course. For historical and technical reasons, the argument that animal biology should be the first course in sequence was compelling, and as a matter of fact, most students took animal biology (Bio 102) in the fall semester.

The Botany department thus maintained an opposition to any kind of sequencing or integration of the two courses, as a survival matter, because it felt it would lose students and a recruitment opportunity with a prerequisite system. It persisted in this position until it was forced to integrate with the Zoology department in the 1990s. After that an "integrated" first year major's course was developed, but there was a vestige of the old conflict buried in its structure. In the first semester, cell and molecular biology were covered, as well as genetics. Biology specific to animals was also taught. In the second semester, ecology and evolution and plant biology were covered. It was an unwritten understanding that a botanist would always teach the second semester, even though any competent biologist should have been able to teach EITHER semester of a first year course. The objective had morphed from maximizing enrollments, to preserving teaching slots for botanists.

Chapter 12
Never Invest in Anything That Eats

Based on my years at URI, I'd say the ratio between the ease for getting money for capital expenses to getting money for maintenance and repairs was maybe 5 to 1. This was at least in part because in the culture of academia, it is much sexier (and easier) to get a grant for $2 million in equipment than to push through an increase in the internal maintenance budget of $100K. One of the main reasons for the relative attractiveness of acquiring capital assets versus maintenance services is that capital requests, if they are made to granting agencies, carry overhead money, up to 60% of the capital request that can be used in a discretionary way by the administration. Maintenance dollars, however, come out of the general college administration budget, which is held with the strength of The Hulk's grip.

I found dozens of letters to administrators in my files, begging for money to preserve our capital investments in equipment and facilities, but their message almost always fell on deaf ears.

Another policy which defied common sense was the practice, related to "zero base budgeting" where if you were, say, a department chair, and were really frugal and diligent about not wasting money in the current fiscal year, your reward was that your budget was decreased in the following year, the reasoning being apparently that you didn't really need the money in the first place. Once having been burned this way, the observant chair would see that there was no point in trying to *save* money while doing the department's business. What you really wanted to do is *overspend* your budget, so you could put in a better claim for more money next year. This practice, I am happy to say, has largely disappeared.

In 1997 I wrote a letter to RI Senator Jack Reed concerning the fact that it was relatively easy to request and receive federal funds for purchase of expensive advanced technology for teaching purposes, but virtually impossible to request funds from the same source for maintenance and repair. I developed a table to show how "hi-tech" projection equipment for a new auditorium compared and contrasted with old-fashioned equipment. The dollar costs today would be different, but the ratios would be about the same.

	Conventional Overhead Projector	Video/computer projector
Initial cost	$500	$18,000
Useful life	15 years	7 Years
Annual bulb cost	$40	$250
Annual alignment	---	$500
Typical annual service/ repair	$30	$150
Lifetime capital cost/year	$33	$2,571
Lifetime maint./repair cost	$1,050	$6,300
Lifetime maint./year	$70	$900

I suggested to Senator Reed that grants for educational technology include a set-aside, or reserve to take care of expensive maintenance during the life of the equipment, a trust fund essentially, and that these funds be protected from "raids" by college administrators desperate for funds for routine operating expenses. To my knowledge, this wasn't done, at least before my retirement in 2010.

In preparation for this section, I browsed through the on-line sites of a number of federal agencies that make grants to higher education, and a quick skim suggested that it is no easier today to get maintenance funds from federal agencies than it was 20 years ago.

Chapter 13
Declining Performance of Freshmen

In 1983, I wrote a letter to the then-Academic Vice President that graphically illustrated the single thing which has had the most profound influence on the nature and character of URI since I began my tenure there. That factor was the gradual proportional erosion of state support of the institution from about 75% of total expenses when I came in 1969, to less than 8% in 2010.This change was due to a tremendous increase in expenses, rather than a reduction of state contribution. This forced the university to develop and promote other sources of revenue to keep the doors open. This necessity has changed almost everything about the place, mostly (in my view) to the negative.

My faculty colleagues and I bitched and whined about these changes for decades, but now from the perspective of a little distance, and having had a taste of the life of an administrator for the three years that I served as Chair of Biological Sciences, I have a lot more sympathy for the folks who had to run the show under those circumstances. Yes, they had to do a lot of unpleasant things, but options are limited when demands for services go up and revenues from the traditional source don't match. You can only ask people to do more for less for so long–pretty soon you start getting less for less.

There was a wonderful example of this a number of years ago. The administration building parking lot would normally empty out around 4:30. Then we started getting all the good soldier requests. Pretty soon, there were more and more cars staying later and later, until it was not uncommon to see the lot still pretty full around 6:30. Then I guess the requests to do more for less finally passed some sort of tipping point, and people eventually said, "They don't pay me enough to do this." In a fairly short period of time, the lot was back to being empty at 5:00.

A state university has three main sources of money for operations; the state, students' tuition, and something called overhead. If a faculty member gets a grant or contract from an outside entity to do research, or provide a service, the university takes a cut from the proceeds. In theory, this compensates the university for the expenses involved in the work; bookkeeping, building maintenance, etc., that the university wouldn't have to provide if the professor didn't have the grant or contract. Now comes Secret Number One.

61

In many cases, the amount collected for overhead amounts to far more than the actual expenses incurred. The surplus goes into the general university kitty. It also converts the rigid and specific expenditure specifications of the grant into discretionary funds administered by college administrators. This provides an almost invisible way that congress can provide direct support to colleges, something that has always been legislatively controversial. Given that overhead essentially represents something very much like profit, the less a state directly provides to the general revenue of the university, the greater the pressure on faculty to develop outside sources of funding, and conserve existing revenue. This has led to a number of far-reaching impacts.

Tuition used to be an insignificant source of revenue. The university could set reasonably high standards for admission and retention, and if significant numbers of students couldn't cut it; so be it. However, the need for more tuition revenue creates an Alice-in-Wonderland situation.

When I came to URI, there were very few out of state students, and the admission standards for out-of-staters were much higher than for Rhode Islanders. The idea for this difference seemed to be that the good out-of-state students could act as stalking horses for the in-state students, stimulating them to better performance. It was true that a disproportionate number of students getting "A's" in my first-year courses were out-of-staters, even though their numbers were much smaller than those of the in-staters.

With the lackadaisical increase in state support, the dramatic increase in expenses due to overbuilding, and the relative ease of raising out-of-state tuition (compared to in-state tuition), the proportion of out-of-state students gradually increased so that now it approaches parity.

Out-of-state students whose parents could pay full tuition without financial aid became fiercely fought-over commodities in the New England state universities. But admission officers were faced with a paradox. Affluent out-of-state parents wanted their kids to attend "selective" universities for their snob value. But if the university was REALLY selective, their academically indifferent kid might not be able to make the cut. So that started admission offices and universities dancing a very complicated jig that required a certain amount of, ah, not *LYING*, exactly, but a bit of creative obfuscation. The recent (2019) scandals about bought admission to elite universities show that the issue is still alive and nationwide, and is not confined to 2nd- and 3rd- tier institutions. This leads us to a letter I wrote to the academic VP.

I started teaching the non-majors intro bio course in 1969, but in 1975, I was "promoted" to the major's course, Zoology 111, which was considered more rewarding to teach, because there were fewer of the walking brain dead to deal with. It takes a couple of years for an instructor to get the "feel" for a big class; what works and what doesn't, how much reading the students will do, how fast they can keep up in lecture, how well they do on exams, etc. After that, unless there are fundamental changes, you'll get pretty much the same class averages on exams from year to year, unless the demographics somehow change. Zoology 111 had stabilized toward the end of the '70s, but in the first three years of the '80s, the bottom started to fall out of class performance, as outlined in the letter to the veep. Without changing the requirements to pass, the failure rate went from 10–15% a semester to 43% – almost *triple* in five years.

What the hell was happening? Were my lectures getting worse? Were my exams getting harder? I was going crazy.

I called in the instructional development program to see if my lecturing quality had decreased. I showed old and new exams to colleagues, who were asked if the new exams were harder for some reason. Nothing jumped out.

I finally gave up, gathered my materials, and made an appointment with the Dean of Admissions. I explained the problem, and asked him straight out if we had lowered our admission standards, to get more out-of-state full tuition paying students. He said flat out, "No."

So I took him aside, and explained that if we really were dealing with a different breed of student, I could change my teaching methods (without lowering the standards), and help keep more of this marginal group (if indeed, they were marginal) without debasing the value of a good grade. He then said something I've never forgotten.

"We have not lowered our admission requirements," he said flatly. "However, we have *revised our concept of scholastic excellence.*"

I was in awe. I realized that I was in the presence of a genius. If this guy had gone to a major advertising agency, or Washington, he could have made a fortune. This was when extracurricular activities, sports, community service, etc. started counting seriously in admission decisions. Armed with this knowledge, I was now in a position to try to do something about the situation.

Chapterlet 5 · Grad School 1

In Rhode Island, where I worked for 41 years, "I know a guy" was a dominant factor in much of the culture, including government. Who you knew was almost as important as what you knew. As I discovered when I prepared to graduate from Berkeley and started looking for grad schools, it was also important in the world of science.

Working in the Museum of Vertebrate Zoology gave me an incalculable advantage over somebody who just had outstanding grades. Because it was literally my job to do favors and run chores for people, including world-famous scientists, I was able to ask for advice, and receive help when I starting looking for grad schools.

For family reasons, I wanted to stay close to home, and San Francisco State University was right across the bay. I had abandoned my first love, reptiles, and was now firmly committed to birds. As it happened, one of the most distinguished ornithologists in the United States, Robert I. Bowman, was on the faculty at SF State. Bowman was the foremost living expert on the birds of the Galapagos Islands. These birds formed the basis for Darwin's "Theory of Evolution by Means of Natural Selection."

Bowman knew several of the scientists at the MVZ who also had international reputations, and when it came to my grad school application, he just called a couple of his buds, and I was in.

I was at State from '62–'64, which was just before the strike and demonstrations of '68 that essentially shut the place down. The science departments mostly stayed away from these activities, but they made going to the student union a lively experience sometimes.

In nuclear physics, the principle "like attracts like" does not apply, but it seems to work in people. I was already showing signs of eccentricity, and SF State was full of eccentrics except they were much brighter than I was. One such was Jack Tomlinson, and he provides a good example of how the atmosphere around colleges was different then.

Jack was the World's Foremost Authority on the Burrowing Barnacles, an obscure group of animals that may be of interest to maybe three or four people around the world. What made Jack so fascinating was that in addition to the burrowing barnacles, he knew a little bit about almost everything, and during his seminar courses that supposedly were about invertebrate animals, Jack would wander off into philosophy, history, psychology, economics, and somehow tie them all together. His seminar was about the invertebrates, but I doubt that we spent more than two days talking about backboneless animals—the rest was about the nature of the universe. I probably learned more useful (and profound) information from Tomlinson than anyone else. Today, I'm sure Jack would be in hot water for not following his course outline.

SF State widened my horizons about the breadth of human nature. I took a grad lab course in vertebrate reproduction. We had to do some rather delicate surgery on rats, and we were informed by the instructor that if our "patients" weren't happy and healthy after their procedure, neither would be our grade.

I had a lab partner who was rather famous around the department, but I wasn't aware of it at the time. She called herself a feminist, but was hardly a good example. She was also an enthusiast for Israel. I'll call her Sarah Msuge. She told me at our first meeting that her overall mission, and the reason she took the course was because her goal was to devise a way to have reproduction without sex. As I discovered, she was the only grad student in the history of the Biology Department to have received an "F" in research from her own major professor.

Sarah and I got to know each other pretty well because after we did the procedure on our rats, for the first day, we had to check up on them in the animal room once every 4 hours. That meant that Sarah and I sometimes got some quality alone time together at 2 AM in the rat room.

Sarah was a yakker, and the minute we walked in the room she started in on how she was being persecuted by everybody. I should add that she was proud of the fact that to show alliance with the poor, she had one set of clothes that were black and looked like a tent, and had worn them since the beginning of the semester, which by now was a long time ago, maybe months. I had to climb a ladder to get to the rack where our rat had his bedroom, and Sarah stayed on the ground taking the notes. The minute I got to the top of the ladder, she fired up on all engines. She was being attacked because she was a woman, and women were powerless in today's corrupt society. She was being attacked because she was a Jew, and Jews had throughout history been persecuted. She was being tormented because she was an activist, and they were being punished for being a threat to The Man.

I couldn't take it any longer, and yelled at her, "Sarah! The chair of the department is a woman. Your own major professor is a Jew. Half the grad students in the department belong to SDS. Yes, nobody likes you, but it's because you talk constantly, insult everybody, don't know what you're talking about, make other people do your work, never change your clothes, and smell like a dead horse in a stable."

She looked at me for a moment, then said, "Oh, Frank, if only I could believe that!"

Chapter 14
Loaves and Fishes

It didn't take long for me to discover that my *actual* job in these big courses was that of a gold miner. A gold miner scoops up a big pan of gravel from the river, and starts sloshing it around with water. Somewhere in all that gravel, he hopes there are some gold nuggets, which he can separate out. However, when he starts out, he doesn't know where the precious nuggets are, so he has to treat each of the little bits in the pan the same way, until the nuggets make themselves visible. However, over the course of time, I discovered that the proportion of gravel to nuggets in my gold pan had increased. There were more and more students in my intro class who were clueless about the requirements of college science courses, and how to study and time budget for them. After it became clear that for economic reasons, URI was admitting students that would never been admitted ten years prior, and that this situation was not likely to change, except in a negative direction, I then made a decision to try, as an experiment, to knock the failure rate in Zoology 111 down WITHOUT lowering the academic standards. The failure rate had steadily climbed from 10-15% in 1975 to a horrendous 43% by 1984. It wasn't any fun teaching a class like that. When you're trying to make education both profitable AND enjoyable for your students, it's hard to do when nearly half your class is looking forward to the possibility of an "F."

I decided to make a radical restructuring of the course. Both then and now I realized that if I were at a different stage of my career, or in a different field of study, the changes would be likely to adversely affect my professional life, because they were so time consuming. However, I was already a full professor; no place to go there. I was in an area of research that didn't require grant money, so I didn't have to worry about losing grant-preparation time (interestingly, when I started my career, the fact that I could do international-quality, good-publicity-generating research without outside money was considered to be a plus. Toward the end of my career, this had changed to the view that I wasn't "pulling my weight," because I wasn't seeking grant money, even though I didn't need it for my research). The pursuit of overhead was now more important than the work itself.

I outlined the specific changes I proposed to make in a letter to the Dean of Arts and Sciences in 1985. I indicated that I viewed these changes as a kind of experiment to see if a difference in teaching approach would make a difference in outcome with this new generation of students.

The major changes were as follows: 1. Institution of recitation and drill sections for the lecture and reading. Handled by the teaching assistants and myself. 2. Institution of a mandatory, 3-hour study skills workshop for all students who fail an exam. Handled by myself. 3. Institution of a computerized grade-tracking system. This would let me follow the weekly progress of each student in the laboratories. This should give early warning of potential failures. 4. Extra TA training in educational psychology and learning theory. 5. Preparation of extra practice questions and written homework. 6. Automatic calling in of students in trouble to discuss their difficulties. 7. Making of a video on study habits to be shown at the beginning of the semester.

I calculated that these steps would take an additional 95 hours for the course instructor (me) and an additional 15 hours each for the TA's during the course of a semester.

I concluded the letter to the Dean by saying, "I plan to resume my normal fraction of time devoted to Zoo 111 in the Spring semester—I cannot defer the needs of my 5 grad students, other courses, and a heavy research and writing schedule indefinitely. If these measures are successful, however, the University will at least have an idea of the kind of effort required to deal with our New Breed of students—and get them through successfully."

After the dust had settled, the two most effective changes were a mandatory study skills workshop the students had to attend at the beginning of the semester, and the fact that any student who flunked the first exam HAD to make an appointment to see me personally and explain; A) Why they thought they flunked, B) What they proposed to change to make sure it didn't happen again, and C) What I could do to help them. They each had eight minutes to do this. If they didn't come to see me; automatic flunk.

Typically, I'd have to see more than 100 students in the two weeks after the exam. The first students to come in were terrified. They had heard about the Evil Prof. Heppner, who was rapidly gaining the sobriquet "Dr. Death." After I'd seen a couple of dozen students and word passed around, the students started to thank me at the end of their interview. This was the only lecture course they'd taken as freshmen where a senior professor had actually taken a *personal* interest in them, even if it was a version of "tough love."

Bottom line? It worked. In three years the failure rate dropped from 43% to 24%. I reported on these results in another letter in 1989 to the

Dean. However, I didn't recommend these techniques for the faculty at large, especially younger faculty in light of "the current climate," which I didn't specify. The Dean sent me a nice reply, in which he also referred to my mention of "the current climate." What we were both talking about was the massive increase in pressure on faculty and mid-and-lower level administrators to crank out more grant proposals, and net more overhead. A "productive" tenure-track faculty member in that sense would have very little time for personal interactions with large numbers of freshmen.

However, by the late '00s, a new buzzword, *retention*, gained currency, and after some calculations, it seemed to me that extra time spent teaching, especially in big classes, could have a substantial economic payback, and I suggested as much in a 2009 article in *Chronicle for Higher Education*[1].

However, another juggernaut was beginning to roll down the hill that would eventually enable the failure rate to be reduced WITHOUT extra faculty time and effort, and the only casualty to be crushed under the wheels of this juggernaut was academic standards. We'll look at this more closely in the next chapter.

---

[1] *On the bottom line, good teaching tops good research*, March 13 2009 55:A72.

Chapter 15
Gosh, Mom, I Got an *A!* Awesome*!*

It is almost laughably easy to manipulate the grading system of a college class so that one produces a higher fraction of good grades than before the adjustment. A bit of skill is required to make the action invisible, but the stakes are so high now, in terms of "retention" of students, that "grade inflation" has become widespread in college.

The basic issue is bald and simple. If you have spent a great deal of time and energy recruiting a marginal student because you either need his/her parents' money, or to make your diversity numbers look better, all that time and effort is wasted if the student flunks out, or does so poorly that he or she transfers to another institution. If you can lower your academic standards in a class so that a higher fraction of students do well than they did before *while making the changes invisible*, almost everybody is happy. The kid is happy. The kid's parents are happy. The financial office is happy. The recruiting office is happy. The legislature is happy. The only parties who are *unhappy* are the professors of the next course in sequence, who had sort of counted on the students actually learning something in the first course, and society at large when it discovers that students graduating with honors can't either write or spell their names.

The easily detectable ways of improving the grades in a class are to switch to grading on a "curve," which does not mean necessarily that if you got an "A" you actually learned a tangible amount of the subject, but means instead that you were the best of a bad lot. Or, you can change the dividing line between grades. If a student used to have to get a 90% to get an "A," now maybe all that's needed is an 85%.

Those are no good because they are too obvious. The easiest, best way to make sure you distribute more good grades is to just make the questions easier. Nobody is going to check your old exams, because; A) Nobody wants to *know* that there has been grade inflation in your class, and B) "Easy" is so subjective and relative, that you'd have to be a teacher of the subject to detect the change.

That inflation has taken place in college is indisputable. URI's Honors Program, which is supposed to be "selective" had to raise the minimum gradepoint from 3.0 to 3.4 because so many students had 3.0s. In 2018, about a third of all URI students were on the Dean's List. Having taught honors students for many years, I can confidently say that the increase in average grade point is not because the newer students are in general actually better.

Being a self-righteous SOB who believed in high, fixed standards, I was reasonably contemptuous of instructors who diluted their academic integrity. However, I was highly sympathetic to young instructors who were under tremendous administrative pressure to be "productive" in their classes, meaning hardly any grades below C–. Then, to my horror, in casually looking over my own exams from decades past, I discovered that I had gradually over the years become an inflater myself! Good God, how did this happen to me, an ardent high-standards guy?

I think I now know the answer. It is difficult to teach a class where the students know, or think they know, that there is a pretty good chance that the SOB instructor is going to give them a bad grade. Especially if you are the only one of their instructors who is "old fashioned" in that way. Walls go up, lecture attendance goes down, and worst of all, they don't laugh at your jokes any more. So very gradually, subconsciously, and unintentionally, you start giving easier and easier questions, so that your average doesn't go down, but ideally goes up, and your students will be happier. The process is so slow you're not even aware that it has happened unless you do the exercise of going through old exams.

I tried an experiment. I found a non-majors intro Biology final exam from 1973. The course was a kind of a biological Rocks for Jocks. Following is a question from that exam:

> 53. *Why does exposure to some diseases, for example, mumps, produce a subsequent immunity? (Correct answer letter italicized)*
>
> *A.* Previous exposure to the organisms producing the disease results in the production of lymphocytes which can produce antibodies specific to that organism.
> B. The structure of the organism producing the disease is "remembered" by the brain, thus when the body is exposed to the organism again, the brain sends instructions to the anti-body producing organs to make the appropriate antigens.
> C. When the organisms circulate in the blood, they pass through the liver, where their structure is analyzed by the liver cells. These cells manufacture antigens, which are

stored in the liver. When the individual is again exposed to the organisms, the liver releases all the stored antigens to the disease.

D. The immunity is produced by cells lining the walls of the intestine. When the disease organisms enter the body, they are scanned by these intestinal cells, which make a template of their structure, which is used to manufacture antigens when, or if, cells of the disease producing organism pass through the intestine again.

E. None of the above.

(Note that the correct answer is not the longest one, which is the usual key to answering multiple-choice exams where you are clueless about the answer.)

The next question is from the premed intro biology final exam from 2007. Take a look at the answers. The old non-major's ones are longer, more involved, and involve some thinking. The new premed questions are much shorter, and primarily are looking for definitions; no thinking involved. The averages were about the same.

13. The physical appearance of an organism for a given trait is termed:
      A) genetics.
      B) dominance
      C) synapsis
      D) genotype
      E) phenotype

What should be the reader's conclusion after reading this chapter?
      A. You can't trust letter grades to mean anything any more.
      B. Letter grades aren't comparable. One instructor's "A" is another's "C."
      C. The higher the stakes for the institution, the higher its grades are likely to be.
      D. All of the above.

The first record I could find of my "alerting" university administration that something was happening with student performance in demanding science courses was in 1983. In the light of subsequent events, I now suspect that my good citizenship was not necessary; the administration well knew that admission "standards of scholastic excellence" had changed in order to draw in more full-tuition paying students. As senility closes in, I have become more phlegmatic about it. Those old-time administrators couldn't really do anything different; the university needed the money, and they couldn't tell anybody about it because that would have hurt recruiting.

Nonetheless, as one who really loved to teach those big classes full of freshmen, it was enormously frustrating to have to deal with students who were so unprepared that they were essentially doomed, despite your best teaching efforts, unless the standards were jiggered.

Most beginning college professors who actually *want* to teach (as opposed to accepting teaching as the price of doing scholarly work) have the naive belief that if they just work hard enough, they can help *all* their students. Today, this belief lasts until they finish their first semester with a really large class. The paradigm then shifts. You are now a first responder, reporting to the scene of a disaster, and you have to perform triage.

There's nothing you can do for the real bottom of the class, the ones who have a 7th grade reading ability, or no real desire to be in college. For them, you shrug your shoulders, offer help if they want and ask for it, and move on to the next group. The really good students don't need your help; they need your *inspiration*. So you tell them about all the cool stuff you do, the headhunters you've met, and offer to let them work in your lab. The ones in the middle—those are the ones you can really reach. Through your efforts, you can help a kid who otherwise would have gotten a "D" to get a "C," or who would have gotten a "C" to get a "B." Needless to say, this takes an enormous amount of time, effort, and dare I say it—skill.

A 1998 letter to the Arts and Sciences Dean sings the same old song, but introduces a new chorus. It seems that with changes in society, parenting, and early education, most of my freshmen in that era *thought they were A students*, and demanded that they be treated as such. They were clearly among the first products of the "Self-esteem Movement" which really started in a big way in California in the '70s and '80s, and has been derisively called the "Participation Trophy Generation." Now, mercifully, with bad times, there are signs that it may be dying out, but—

I had a wonderful example of this in the early '00s. Technically, a Dean could not *order* a faculty member to talk to a disgruntled parent about a student's grades. Also, a teacher couldn't discuss a student's grade with ANYONE without the student's permission.

A couple of days after the semester was over, I got a call from my Dean *inviting* me to come in and meet an upset parent and discuss her son's final grade. That was fine with me, so I gathered some documents, and strolled over to the Dean's office at the agreed upon time.

When I walked in the office, Mrs. Outraged was standing in front of the Dean's desk, berating her in a voice that I remember to this day. I should mention that her son was sitting in a chair as close to the door as possible, and doing his best to look invisible. Mom didn't look at me.

"How DARE you employ a person calling himself a teacher who *fails 60 percent of his students! Who last gave an A in 1996. And was so bad a teacher that you wouldn't even let him in front of a class last year!!!!!*"

I could see that the kid's eyes were rolling around in panic, checking for exits. I didn't have to be a genius to figure out where Mom's information came from.

When she finished, the Dean turned to me and asked if I would like to respond.

I brought out my folder full of documents. "Thank you, Dean. Perhaps I could refine the information you have a bit. Here are the grade distributions for the class your son was in for the past 5 years. As you can see, the failure rate is not 60%, but 10–15%. The percentage of A's is about the same, so over the past five years, there are hundreds of students who have received A's. And, it is true that I wasn't teaching this class last year. I had received a Fulbright fellowship to represent the United States to the Ministry of Education of His Majesty the Sultan of Brunei and was thus in Southeast Asia for a year. And now as to your son's performance in the course, Sean, may I show your mother your scores?"

I thought Sean was going to dissolve in a puddle of sweat, but he reluctantly nodded yes.

"Hmmm. Let's see. Sean, it appears that you didn't go to half the labs, so we don't have quiz scores, you didn't turn in your term paper, you missed the first mid-term and didn't make it up, and your final exam score was 47%. Under the circumstances, I had no choice but to issue an F. Any other questions, Madam?"

I didn't really expect an *apology*, but Mom just pumped herself up, said "We'll see about this!" and stormed out the door, Sean following closely behind. We never heard from her again.

It was about at this point that my student evaluations started to become bimodal. The students who really were old-fashioned A students LOVED the big courses. Many of the others, however, thought I was Lucifer, and a word not used much by anyone older than about eight, *unfair*. Unfair in the kid sense that he didn't get what he wanted, rather than some sense of equity.

As I demonstrated earlier, part of the problem was addressed when I unknowingly made the course easier. I never really drew any significant static from administration for being a tough grader, but I suspect that younger faculty, especially untenured ones, would receive a nice chat from a dean if they graded as I did 25 years ago.

Chapter 16
Boy, Did I Get This One Wrong
(But, Was I Ever a Prophet!)

By the early '80s, financial crises in colleges were becoming the norm. I'd been teaching big courses with laboratories for a dozen years, and it seemed like it was getting harder and harder to teach them with each passing year. In the laboratories we were cutting back on activities that required consumables, and it finally got to the point where I had to teach a first year lab course for today's equivalent of about $12 per student per semester.

The first record I could find in my correspondence of a reference to computer-assisted instruction (CAI) was in 1981. At that time, CAI referred mostly to mainframe-connected terminals—Apple had launched its extremely aggressive marketing policies for elementary and high schools around 1979, but hadn't yet had much of an impact on colleges.

In reading over the correspondence in the dossier, it appears that I was advocating the use of computers in laboratory classes not necessarily because they were better than conventional physical equipment but because of budget constraints; we simply couldn't teach using the conventional method any more, and it was probably cheaper to make a capital request for classroom computers, and eliminate the routine lab expenses, which had to come out of department funds every year.

I *did* say that "CAI has been shown to be at least as effective as conventional teaching." I'm now embarrassed to admit that I claimed this—at the time, there was practically no evidence of the effectiveness of CAI *beyond its novelty value.* And, about the only things available for computers in biology education then were drill programs, and "educational game" programs with crude graphics.

Experience has now suggested that computers *are* helpful in science classes, but not in the universal way we once thought was possible. There are several issues. If the major value is novelty, what happens when the novelty wears off? "Graphics competition" is a second area. About 15 years ago, both to cut costs, and eliminate complaints from animal-rights activists, the Department of Biological Sciences replaced its animal-based physiology experiments with computer simulations. Surprisingly, the students hated them, and for a rather odd reason. It is staggeringly expensive to develop *good* computer graphics. Grand Theft Auto V cost about $265 million to develop and market. The early physiology simulations were crude, simplistic, and by comparison with what the students were already used to from their video games, boring. The current classroom simulations are still 2–3 generations behind what is available in the game and video market, and with today's limited attention spans, as the Rhode Islanders say, fuggedabout it.

However, the computer is now firmly ensconced in education, and I don't think we'll ever go back. However, there are still some rather large unanswered questions that nobody, especially those involved in marketing computers for education, seem to want to raise. For example, there are quite a few studies that indicate that people read more slowly, and make more errors when reading off a screen, rather than off paper. What would be the overall impact on education if it took 5% longer to read documents from a screen instead of old-fashioned paper?

At the present, there have been hundreds of studies on the benefits of computer use in classrooms, and the results are at best ambiguous. This is especially disturbing when you consider how much money has been spent by schools and colleges in facilitating computer use in classrooms. There has been enormous marketing hype to get computers in schools, and that factor needs to be plugged into evaluating any individual study. In the last days of my career as a big class (300+ students) lecturer, the university allowed the use of laptops and handheld devices in lecture halls. I very quickly learned that my eye contact with students started to drop precipitously as more and more of them brought their screens into lecture. The reason advanced by the university for this permission was that students tended not to make handwritten notes any more, and maybe if they could use a laptop, or something like, they would take better notes.

From the podium, of course, I couldn't see what was on their screens. So I asked one of my teaching assistants to stand in the back of the auditorium, and scan the screens. What was on them? Unh, not exactly notes. Depending on student gender, either *World of Warcraft,* or *The Sims 2.* Now, what students mostly seem to have on their in-class notebooks (if they have anything pertaining to the class at all) is Powerpoints downloaded from the lecturer. With the hypnotic effect of the social media and the ascendancy of the phone over the laptop, more recently even those Powerpoints are joining the Mario Bros in computer limbo.

Chapterlet 6 · Grad School 2, Davis

The two years at San Francisco State went quickly, and it was time to look for someplace to get a Ph.D. I still wanted to stay reasonably close to San Francisco, and the University of California–Davis immediately popped up. Davis was the old Aggie school, but in recent years had received national prominence in Zoology. Bob Bowman had heard about a new faculty member named William J. Hamilton III who was both interested in birds, and kind of weird—both requirements for a future major professor for me.

I hopped up to Davis and chatted with Bill and a couple of his students. I found that he was the son of a distinguished Cornell scientist named William J. "Wild Bill" Hamilton Jr. As it turned out, like father, like son. *My* Bill became the only man I ever knew to have been bitten in the crotch by a zebra, but more about that later.

Bill had been in the service during the Korean War, and had won a large sum of money playing poker. When he came to Davis just the year before I came, he invested heavily in Davis orchard land, which almost immediately began to appreciate, so Bill financed much of his own research, something almost unheard of today. Bill's initial interest at Davis was in the enormous flocks of starlings that roosted at night near the cattle feed lots, but didn't remain there for the day. They would sometimes fly out 50 miles from the roost to feed in the fields surrounding the roost. But why? Why waste all that time and energy flying that far, if you could feed closer to the roost? That was the first scientific problem I worked on with Bill at Davis.

To try to answer that question, Bill's students would drive out from the roost at first light, stop at 10-, 20-, 30-, 40-, and 50-mile intervals and census the bird density at each distance. What we found was a kind of biological equivalent of the Nash equilibrium in game theory. If a bird stayed close to the roost, he wouldn't have to expend much energy, but since other birds might have the same idea, there would be more competition for food. At greater distances, there was more energy expended, but less competition. So the end result was likely to be the same whatever distance the bird picked.

On one of the early censusing trips, Bill went along with me and another grad student, Jon Planck, on our drive. We traveled through the California Central Valley, which is one of the great bird migration routes of the world. You could see thousands of geese flying overhead. I was fascinated by this, not having seen it in any of my prior residences. Often you would see the birds flying in a vee formation. On one trip, I asked Bill why the birds flew in a vee. He said that the first bird was in effect cleaving a path through the air, allowing the other birds, who might be closely related, to tuck in behind and save energy. Sort of like drafting in stock car racing.

I didn't say anything, but I knew something about stock car racing, and Bill's answer was horsepucky. In stock car racing, you tuck in directly behind the car in front, not to one side. The question was interesting enough that once I had my own lab at URI I started working on it, and 30 years later, I think I came up with the answer. But it all started with Bill.

It was the '60s, and academic society was so different that it's hard to explain from this distance. What was normal or even expected then, is now improper or even illegal today. This is especially true in the social aspects of academia.

Bill was interested in animal behavior, and actually had more in common with many of the faculty in psychology than with the other zoologists. Bill and his grad students were often invited to psych faculty parties, One very distinguished younger psych professor I'll call "Jim" studied sheep sex behavior. Woody Allen's movie "Everything You Wanted to Know About Sex" featuring Gene Wilder and a sheep named Daisy came out only 5 years after I left Davis, so it was in the cultural air.

Jim's research was on male sex performance after fatigue in sheep. He'd put a ram and a ewe in receptive condition into a pen. Ram would instantly come over and get it on with the ewe. Thirty seconds later, he would have at it again. Then a minute later, then two minutes. Five minutes Ten minutes. When he got to a half-hour interval, he'd go over to a corner and look like he was having a near-death experience. But then Jim would take out the original ewe and put in a fresh receptive ewe. Ol' ram was good as new. Thirty seconds, a minute, etc. Needless to say, the randy professors in Jim's department were very interested in his line of research.

Hard as it may be to believe but the *grad students* were sometimes a bit shocked by the *faculty* behavior at these affairs, rather than the other way around. There were sometimes faculty house key exchanges at the end of the parties.

One internationally famous ecologist from Bill's department was extremely shy, and never said anything the parties. He was an outstanding researcher, however, got the psychology research bug from the psych faculty at the party, and was inspired to do a little outside-of-his-discipline research.

He had a gorgeous wife, and he was somehow able to persuade her to be his lab rat, as it were. They bought a series of costumes for her, from very conservative cowgirl, to something that would be at home at the House of Blue Lights. They made a list of the local cowboy bars, and when they had fairly slow nights. He would equip himself with a notebook and stopwatch, she would dress in one of the test costumes, then he and his wife would go into the bar separately, but about at the same time. He would inconspicuously sit at one end of the bar, pull out the notebook and timer, and she would sit at the other. They would both order beers, and he'd start the clock when she got her beer. He'd stop it when the first cowboy came over to proposition her. The idea was to measure the effect of attire on cowboy attraction. I don't think they ever published their results, because human subjects committees were just coming into use, and I think this is one proposed experiment that wouldn't go through.

By the time I finished at Bill's lab, I had five scientific publications, including one in *Science*. I was at Davis for three years, but Bill decided to go to Africa during much of my final year. So I pretty much was on my own. He was in the Sinai Peninsula during the Six-Days War, and refuged in the home of an Egyptian policeman. He went to South Africa to measure the temperature under the black and white stripes on the neck of a zebra using sub-dermal temperature radio transmitters. A ranger shot the zebra with a tranquilizer dart, then Bill stretched out on the ground with the zebra's head in his lap while he inserted the little sensors. For some reason, the zebra woke up quickly, assessed the situation, and gave Bill a stunning bite in the crotch—never knew anyone else who had this experience.

When Bill came back from his year, he looked like Lawrence of California. Hair and beard like Jesus. Aba and thobe gown, sandals. In most jobs, this would have called for a visit from the mental health officials in the personnel office, but Bill brought Davis so much good publicity from his research and many other conservation activities, the almost universal reaction was, "Well, Bill's just being Bill." It did not take long to conclude that a university was a good place for me, but in the next couple of years I saw that success in a university environment could ALSO be found by the opposite of eccentricity—and in the passage of time, that would become the dominant mode in most colleges

Chapter 17
The Road to Hell
is Paved with Good Intentions

I have a theory about federal bureaucracies. They start when someone who has a bit of authority, say a member of Congress, sees some kind of legitimate problem like water pollution. They say quite reasonably, "Something should be done about this." They set up an agency and establish regulations. So far, so good. The first people hired by this agency will tend to be crusaders, and believers in the cause. But then, once the size of the agency passes some tipping point, the new hires are people for whom the job is just a job. And they quickly learn the eternal truth that in a mature bureaucracy, you don't get promoted and get raises by solving the problem you are charged with dealing with. Instead, you advance by expanding the definition of the problem, so more people can be hired (under your direction). This new generation of hires tend to be sticklers for regulatory detail who have no recognition of common sense, because that can't be regulated. Through my career, the influence of these bureaucracies became more pervasive, and ultimately affected the kind and quality of work I could do in both teaching and research, if for no other reason than complying with the regs took so damned much time.

For example, much of my research involved just looking at wild common birds in the field. Some of it I could do just by taking movies of birds landing on feeders around my house. Pretty innocuous, right? However, after 1986, I had to file an application with, and get permission from URI's IACUC (Institutional Animal Care and Use Committee), otherwise known as the Animal Welfare Committee, to watch birds for scientific purposes around my house. I had to appear before the committee and make a presentation explaining why I couldn't obtain the data any other way than by watching the birds. Now, some of these birds, like starlings and domestic pigeons were considered pest species, I could blast them with a shotgun without anybody's permission, but to LOOK at them with science in mind, I had to do the voluminous paperwork. I don't know if the birds could tell the difference between being watched for pleasure, or for scientific purposes, but the animal welfare committee sure could. The current document containing guidelines for obtaining and using permits for scientific studies of birds is 215 pages long. It advises that amateurs shouldn't even bother to apply.

I'll also tell you this story. I've been a photographer since I was 10 years old, and have been exposed to photographic chemicals since that time. Photographers have been using the same chemicals for almost 200 years. Sure, if you took a nice big swig out of a bottle of developer, you might get a tummy ache, but who's going to do that unless they want to commit suicide? A non-photographer is not going to casually walk into a darkroom, look at a bottle, say, "Gee, maybe it's gin!" and take a big swig. Nevertheless the chemicals ARE poisonous, and thus fell under the influence of the EPA and OSHA. Photographic darkrooms were like heaven and a full-employment program to people working for those agencies.

I was involved with the Zoology Department's darkroom, and had my own darkroom in my lab. Every new stupid time-consuming regulation that came down the road I cursed—but obeyed. Pretty soon the darkrooms were full of warning signs.

Well, hell. As long as I was filling up the darkroom door with mandated warnings (which were so numerous, they practically guaranteed that nobody would read them), I decided to post a few additional, helpful warnings. We wash film with water, so I posted the government MSDS (chemical information sheet) for water, LC26750, which specified that if you spilled water on your skin, as a first aid measure, you should wash the exposed area with soap and water. I further cautioned that users should not exhale in the darkroom because human exhalate exceeded EPA standards for CO_2 greenhouse gas emissions. Just trying to help.

Everything was fine until the EPA inspector came around. He looked at my bottles and my records. So far, everything good and shipshape. Then he looked at the door. His mouth shrank down to the size and shape of a Cheerio. Then he said to me in this dead flat voice, "You're mocking the regulations."

Cheerily, I replied, "Yes, Sir! But the last time I looked, the First Amendment of the Constitution of the United States says that I can mock them as long as I follow them."

Ooooo, he didn't like that! For the next several years, as long as I was on his route, I got the full mirror-under-the-counter, line-by-line microscopic inspection of the books treatment. This ultimately proved to be more of a pain in the ass to me then the pleasure derived from extending the guy's workday, so I eventually took the offending signs down. I always felt guilty, though. What if somebody spilled water on his hand, and I didn't have the appropriate first-aid technique posted?

I just looked up the MSDS for water, released in 2014. Still recommends washing with soap and water if you spill it on your skin.

Chapter 18
Longest Running Civil Lawsuit
in Rhode Island History

Colleges and universities can provide almost endless examples of bureaucracies run amok, but in their daily doings, universities must also interact with OTHER bureaucracies that, each in their own way, provide food for the connoisseur of waste motion and energy.

In the early 1970s, when I was much crazier than I am today, I had a grad student, Dave, who was even crazier than I was. He was a descendant of the commander of the USS *Constitution* during the war with the Barbary Pirates. Like his ancestor, Dave was a man of the sea, and an expert small boat handler. He was the only guy I ever knew who was tossed out of West Point for fighting.

Dave and I came up with a research plan to study the populations of feral pigeons living in the abandoned Plum Beach lighthouse near the Jamestown bridge. It meant that every two weeks, we would get in my 17-foot Boston Whaler which was docked in Wickford harbor in Narragansett Bay, and motor out to the lighthouse. It was a round trip of about 9 miles. When I say "every two weeks" that's just what I mean—storm, snow, ice, summer, winter. No difference. Most of the time, we could tie the boat up to the old abandoned dock at the lighthouse, but if the weather was too rough, I'd get as close as I could to the leeward side of the structure, and Dave would jump from the bow to the usually-icy rocks.

The lighthouse was a shithole. Literally. It had been abandoned in 1940, the windows had broken out, and pigeons had moved in to establish a colony. There were no nest predators, like rats, in the lighthouse so the pigeons were free to breed without restriction—that was what made it interesting to study.

Colonial pigeons build their nests on the ground, and when the shit piles up, they build new nests on top of the old dung-encrusted ones. By the time we started our study, there was 1-2 feet of aromatic pigeon crap on the ground. Now, Dave and I were crazy, but we weren't *crazy*, because pigeon guano is known to harbor diseases, so we wore appropriate protective gear; mask, gloves, eye protection, etc.

The lighthouse was owned by the ancestor of today's Department of Environmental Management of the State of Rhode Island. We had obtained permission from them to do the study, and when we discovered the condition inside, we wrote to them and said that the interior was a severe health hazard, due to the strong possibility of a trespasser contacting something called histoplasmosis, and told them we were putting a padlock on the only door, and sent them a copy of the key. We also mounted a "skull and crossbones" sign, with an explanation, outside the door.

When we finished the study a couple of years later, we wrote a termination letter to the state, reiterating the hazard, and advising that they weld the door shut. We then moved on to other things. Dave became Cap'n Dave of the "Early Bird" a charter fishing boat, and his school year job was teaching high school biology.

A couple of years later, getting ready for the American Bicentennial in 1976, the state decided to paint the exterior of the lighthouse red, white, and blue. They removed our padlock, removed our sign, and hired a painting contractor. A couple of the painters, curious, decided to explore the interior, and why not? Surprise! A couple of years later, one of them developed histoplasmosis, and decided to sue the ass off the state.

An attorney for the state contacted me, must have been the late '70s, and I advised her to settle as fast as she could. The state had been informed of the hazard in writing, had removed the warning signs, removed the lock, and one could argue, knowingly exposed the painters to risk, and there was a detailed paper trail for all of it. Open-and-shut case, and simple justice, by the way.

That's not what happened. The matter got caught up in the internal politics of the agency, and they began a stonewalling process that lasted *more than 20 years!* Their argument was essentially, "Well, yes, the guy got histoplasmosis, he was in the lighthouse full of pigeon shit, the state took down the warning sign, you can get histoplasmosis from pigeon shit, but how do we know that *his* histoplasmosis came from the pigeon shit in the lighthouse? Maybe he got it from the pigeons in Boston Common."

Over the years, I was called in to depose statements a couple of times, and that was very interesting to me, as a scientist, to watch the opposing lawyers. *Neither* of the attorneys were interested in finding out "the truth" as a scientist might—their mission was to win for their client. Almost every time I opened my mouth, there was an objection from one side or the other. In science, suppressing information that would be unsupportive of your hypothesis is a high crime and misdemeanor. In the law, it is apparently SOP.

I sort of lost interest in the case over the decades, but the painter was still alive when the case was finally settled for an undisclosed sum. I really don't know how badly his life was compromised, but it really doesn't matter-justice wasn't done.

Chapter 19
General Education = Full Employment Plan

When I started teaching in the late '60s, research universities often had a lot of relatively small academic departments, like Classics, or Far Eastern Studies. Then, as the economic realities of the '80s began to kick in with a vengeance, number of students enrolled in courses became a new metric for judging the survivability of a small department. Since the yardstick was often number of student credit hours/department/faculty member, it quickly became obvious that if you were a faculty member in a small department with only four or five members, and the measure of central tendency for average number of students in a course was the MEAN, not the median or the mode, one megacourse with thousands of students enrolled would let your department continue to offer the upper division courses that old Prof. Skaalagard loved to teach, like "Runic Literature of the Faero Islands," for the department's three majors. Not incidentally the department would have a shot at holding on to teaching assistantships, and maybe even replacing retiring faculty.

But where to dredge up the hordes of students you needed to do this if you were in a small, specialized department? Most colleges have what is called a "General Education" graduation requirement for undergraduates. Every student has to take a minimum number of credits in each of several broad areas, like "Humanities," "Social Sciences," or "Science." Sometimes, there would be a skills division, like writing. The theory of a general education is wonderful, and I support it absolutely. In practice, campus politics is often more important than good educational intentions in deciding what the exact requirements are.

Most of the mainstream science departments like Chemistry had no problem with enough enrollments to protect their existence. Departments like mine, Zoology/Biological Sciences, had an opposite problem than the one faced by tiny departments. How on earth were we going to handle all our freakin' students? Small departments, however, had a powerful need to hustle up student credit-hours.

Now, if there was a general education requirement that involved most departments in a college, would all the courses a department offered be eligible for Gen Ed credit? For example, were upper division, or advanced courses usually eligible for Gen Ed? No, and this led to more smoke-filled-room, nasty backstage politicking than any area I had anything to do with during my career.

I found in my stored papers two letters addressed to the URI academic vice president around 1990, when revisions to the Gen Ed requirement were being discussed. It appears that I had two main squawks about how the new Gen Ed requirements for students were being set up.

First, I considered a small, hypothetical department in the "Science" Gen Ed area. Students had to take two approved Gen Ed courses in each broad area, but they could take either or both courses in the same department. Let's call our little department the "Department of Fish" in the College of the Environment. Fish had 5 professors, 15 majors, and was expensive to run because of the heavy lab class expenses. Normal class enrollment was about 12 students.

With properties like this, the Department of Fish would be a good candidate for elimination or merger with the "Department of Animals Other than Fish." In either case, jobs and resources would be lost to the faculty members of Fish.

However, if Fish could offer a Gen Ed course that would be enormously popular with undergraduates, and could draw hundreds of students, that would make the AVERAGE enrollment in Fish courses above that needed for survival and resources. So, if Fish could get a course called "Our Friends, the Toadfish" approved by the Gen Ed university faculty committee, that would be like having a key to the life jacket locker on the Titanic, as long as the course drew in hundreds of students, attracted by the possibility of exam questions asking how many legs a tuna had. However to GET a course like that approved by the campus Gen Ed committee might require a bit of wheeling, dealing, and dickering.

Now, that wouldn't be an inherently fatal flaw in the Gen Ed requirement, BUT if there were another small department in the same college facing the same problem as Fish, let's say the Department of Urine and Excretion, it might be tempted to offer a similar first-year lecture course called "The Kidney in Song and Literature." Sounds ridiculous but some of the real courses offered for Gen Ed weren't much different. Being easy, it would attract droves of students. Since the requirement said you only needed two courses in each division, a kid could take Toadfish and Kidneys, and that would be it for his or her science requirement. Not exactly the pathway to broad scientific literacy, or the intention of a General Education requirement. The other flaw with the system was that many departments wanted to maximize the number of courses that their majors took within their own departments, and minimize the number of courses they took out-of-department. In theory, general education courses could not be used for majors' credits, because any student on campus was supposed to be able to take them and do reasonably well, and French majors tended not to thrive in something like premed intro bio. This is why technical majors like mine had two large introductory courses—one for their own and related majors, and another for non-majors. Still, by judicious dickering, some departments, including my own, got their major's intro courses, and even some second-level courses listed under Gen Ed. So that way, a bio major wouldn't have to take anything in a Gen Ed division outside his major, and would still satisfy his Gen Ed requirement. Not the route to a broad education. This policy has, I believe, been addressed in recent years, but was in effect during most of my early days.

Another issue with Gen Ed was the problem of who was going to teach the courses. In theory, these are the hardest classes to teach well, because the students mostly didn't want to be there, and certainly didn't want to work very hard. There were a few oddballs like myself who took this as a personal challenge, and LIKED big gen ed courses but that was atypical. So teaching the intro courses fell to: A) The new hire, B) Somebody on the chair's s–t list, or C) Gypsy, adjunct faculty. We had generally good luck with C, because most of them were fresh out of grad school, enthusiastic, and hadn't yet been beaten down by reality. They quickly learned, however, that being tough on grading earned them the Invitation to Try Other Opportunities.

I think ultimately the reason I squawked about this so much was that I really believed in a traditional liberal education, being an AB myself, and all this political crap essentially defeated the purpose of having a general education requirement by allowing a student to satisfy the Gen Ed requirement by taking a few low-level, but highly specialized easy courses in each division. Too bad.

Chapterlet 7 · Post-doc at the University of Washington

"So," he said, puffing on the ever-present pipe,
"What do you have for me this week?"

In 1967, I went from the barely organized chaos of Bill Hamilton's lab, to become a post-doctoral research fellow in the highly ordered Big Science lab of Donald Farner, at the University of Washington. Don had about 250 scientific publications, was Chair of the Zoology Department, and had been the Dean of the grad school, President of the American Ornithologist's Union, Chair or President of several international biological societies, and had been a Captain in the Navy. His other post-doc and his grad students figured he was also a spook for Naval Intelligence, because whenever he went to scientific meetings in eastern Europe, which was once or twice a semester, about 2 days after he got back, a guy in a suit and brown shiny shoes would show up without an appointment, and Farner would lock himself in his office with him for a couple of hours. All this work didn't faze Don, but I got tired just writing this paragraph.

When I was there Don had 2 post-docs and 5 grad students. He was a big fan of organization, and his day ran something like this: Arrive at lab at 6:00 a.m. 6:00–8:00, do reading of scientific literature. 8:00–9:00, appointments with grad students and post-docs. Grad students got 15 minutes a week, post-docs a half hour. During your time, you were expected to *report* on progress you had made that week. There was no chit-chat. 9:00–12:00, write books and scientific papers. 12:00–12:45, swim at gym pool. 12:45–1:00, lunch. 1:00–5:00, conduct university and department business. 5:00–6:00, attend department seminars. 6:00, depart for home. Home at 6:35, then cocktails (martinis).

The only interruption to this routine was when he traveled, which was every two weeks or so. When this happened, I was in charge of the lab, a non-trivial assignment, because we kept birds in air-conditioned rooms that had to be kept +/- 2.0°. There was an alarm built into the room, and if the temperature started to vary by more than .5°, I had one of the first pagers in Seattle, and I had a half-hour to get to the lab and fix the problem, no matter where I was. I got to know quite a few Seattle cops (and a lot about fixing refrigeration units).

One might ask why on earth anyone would want to be a student in that kind of environment. Simple answer—when you had your allotted time with him, he gave you his *undivided* attention, and all the resources you needed to do your work. In return he expected rigor and thoroughness in your research.

Although post-docs received their fellowships to do research, there was a certain amount of flexibility, and you were allowed to teach courses with the permission of your adviser, in my case, Don Farner. In the Spring of '68, he let me teach Natural History of the Vertebrates, Zoo 362. It turned out that I was younger than quite a few of the students, which was a twist, but it was a lab/field course, so the energy of youth was a real advantage.

One of the valuable lessons teaching this class taught me was that it is very tough to predict how a kid will turn out based on his performance in a college class. One of my students was named "Chad." He was the class clown and official goofball, and I seem to remember that he ended up with a "C," which shows you how good a predictor I am. For some reason I kept in touch with him over the years, and "Chad" ended up being one of the most distinguished wildlife biologists in the Pacific Northwest, and wrote dozens of books, some for National Geographic, and others for Sierra Club.

The Pacific Northwest wouldn't go through its huge boom with the start of 747 production until early '70, so the wild areas like the Olympic Peninsula, the Cascades, and the eastern Washington deserts were still pretty virginal. In the Olympics you could reliably see rare or endangered species on almost every trip. I was also a railroad enthusiast, and the beautiful long-distance trains terminating in Seattle were still operating.

There was a dark, well, not actually dark, more like dim, aspect of working for Don. Let's call her a close relative, but a member of Don's family regarded the grad students and postdocs in the lab as extra household help. When there were leaves to be raked, or snow to be shoveled, a call came in, and we were expected to hustle out to his house to take care of the problem. I remember grumbling about it, and today, it would be unheard of for grad students or post-docs to be taken advantage of in this way, but on the other hand, when your post-doc was up, and it was time to get a regular faculty job, one phone call from Don got you the job. *That* doesn't happen today, either, with all the bureaucracy involved in faculty jobs.

In Spring of '69, Don gave me an opportunity that changed the direction of my life. He gave me a chance to team-teach the big intro Zoology course with an older, experienced teacher named Ken Osterud. Ken was a photographer and showed me that using slides with music was an effective teaching technique. I also got used to speaking before a large group, something that grad students aren't often allowed to do.

I also had one of the finest examples of a kind of experience that you can't have today. People (and comedians) don't often tell story-based jokes today; what you get is mostly one-liner gags from TV and stand-up comedians. But until the '70s or so, jokes were really oral stories, and the idea was to suck the audience into the story until they HAD to find out how it ended—sometimes the buildup would be five–ten minutes. People apparently don't have the patience for this anymore. But back in the day, if you were a good enough story teller, you could build people's interest as you went until they would almost explode with laughter when they heard the punch line.

But there was an evil cousin to the story-type joke. It was called a "Shaggy Dog Story." I don't have enough room to describe it exactly, but you can still look it up on Wikipedia. It really is a kind of practical joke on the listener, and a test of story-telling ability in the teller. What you basically do is tell a long, complicated build up, trying to make the listener salivate in expectation of hearing the punch line, and then JUST as he thinks he's anticipated the punch line—there's no punch line. The dog wasn't really shaggy after all. If the story teller did a good job, the listener would be so impressed by how well you suckered him in, he'd laugh anyway.

Farner had a lab manager who was a salty ex-Navy Chief Bosun's Mate named Bob. He'd been around the world, and wasn't impressed by anything. We used to have a ten-minute coffee break together every couple of days, and we'd talk about our travels and adventures. Somehow the topic, as it does sometimes with men, got around to the best sex act we knew about. There's usually a certain amount of lying involved.

I remembered this "shaggy dog story" somebody got me on, and I thought I'd try my skill on Bob. I told him I had learned about the world's most exciting sex act in Singapore, but it was wildly dangerous and men had died horribly when things went wrong. It was called "The Sleeve Job." Alas, "The Sleeve Job" has disappeared from the net—maybe it's on The Dark Web.

Needless to say, Bob wanted to hear about it. So I started out with me in a bar in Singapore hearing about it, then wandering all over Asia to find someone to give me a Sleeve Job, but somehow, I always just missed. The whole idea was to tell it not as a joke, but a true story.

Since we had only 10 minutes for coffee every day, I'd have to stop the story, and pick it up next time. I could tell I had him hooked and suckered in, so the story got more and more elaborate. I knew I finally had to end it sometime, so I finished up with me in the lobby of the Hilton in Manila, buying a case of Vaseline before I went to meet the most beautiful woman in the world in her suite on the 10th floor.

Bob was, despite himself, on the edge of his seat waiting to find out what the Sleeve Job was. He was practically panting when I finished the story by saying, "She was all ready, but her body was coated with Vaseline, so when I embraced her, she shot out of my arms, over the 10th floor balcony, and fell to her death a hundred feet below. So I *never did* find out what a Sleeve Job was."

He stared at me for about 10 seconds, and then realizing how badly he'd been bamboozled, almost rolled off his chair.

There was an actual value to these joke-telling sessions. The skills involved in telling a good story joke are the same that you need in holding a class's attention. I'm glad I had a chance to practice.

Chapter 20
Reorganization of the Biological Sciences

One of the most complex and contentious events in the life of any large organization is an internal restructuring. URI experienced this when the biological sciences were reorganized, a process that started in the late '80s, and continues to this day. Most of the early faculty and administrative participants are no longer at URI, and I fear that this ancient story will be lost to institutional memory. This would be unfortunate, because I believe the past may well predict the future, and there are profitable lessons here for any institution facing similar changes.

The first major document I found in my old files referring to this matter was dated 1990, and was a letter addressed to the then-Dean of the Graduate School who was chair of an ad-hoc committee called LESTF (Life and Environmental Sciences Task Force). At the time, most of the biological sciences departments were divided between two colleges; Arts and Sciences, which started in 1948 with the awarding of URI's first Bachelor of Arts degree, and Resource Development (the old College of Agriculture, which had morphed into Resource Development in 1968). Resource Development originally included the "practical" departments like Turfgrass Management, Fisheries, and Poultry Science. Zoology and Botany were in Arts and Sciences. URI had started out as the state's agricultural college. There were a few biologists in the College of Oceanography.

There was a predecessor to the turmoil that shortly ensued, and it was experienced by most research universities in the '70s. For lack of a better term, I'll call it the Molecular Wars. E. O. Wilson described it in colorful fashion in his 1994 book, *Naturalist.*

Until the '50s, the study of biology in universities was dominated by organismal biologists; people who studied whole animals and plants, or pieces of animals and plants, as in physiology. Microbiology (bacteria and viruses) had long been parceled separately. Then with Watson and Crick's discovery of the structure of the DNA molecule in 1953, the field of molecular biology experienced a rapid and explosive growth, and was soon competing for resources with organismal biology in traditional biology departments.

When I came to URI in 1969 in the Zoology Department, I was the bird expert. We also had a fish expert, a mammal expert, a reptile expert, an insect expert, and a marine organism expert. Today, the descendant Department of Biological Sciences has NO experts on specific kinds of

101

animals. The victory of molecular biology over organismal biology was total and complete. To be fair, people interested in ecology often have some training in organismal biology, and ecology is well represented in the new College of the Environment and Life Sciences, formed in the '80s.

It was in the '70s that the war began in earnest at URI. As the old specific animal and plant people retired, there were fierce battles over the nature of their replacements. These were not friendly competitions; survival of a world view was at stake, and at times it got downright nasty; so what else is new in Academia? There was a certain amount of mutual contempt. The two camps were called Boots Biologists (because we often worked in the field under rugged conditions) and Labcoat Biologists (who worked in air conditioned labs). The Labcoat Biologists didn't think the Boots Biologists were very smart, and the Boots Biologists didn't think the Labcoat Biologists were very, ah, *manly* (needless to say, in those days, both groups were largely male—the reverse of the situation today).

The earliest document I found relating to this conflict was dated 1983, and it presented a passionate defense for the hiring of a new organismal biologist(s) to replace the now-vanished ones. Some of the flavor of the debate can be gained by the tone of the arguments, which, if I do say so, were rather strident, reflecting the seriousness with which non-molecular faculty regarded the situation. There are a couple of cryptic references. One sentence suggested that "investment in molecular now is like buying Atari stock a month ago." My memory failed me on the significance of this observation, and I had to look it up. It referred to the huge crash in video game stocks starting in 1983, with about 97% of the value of the industry being lost in the space of two years. Clearly, my prognostication that molecular biology would die an early and impoverished death did not suggest a skill in predicting the future.

The second oddity was a curious scrawled notation "he/she" at the top of the typewritten page. I scratched my head over this for a while, but I *think* this may have to do with the fact that gender neutral language was beginning to enter widespread academic consciousness at about that time, and the pronoun "he" that was widely used as a neutral pronoun, depending on context, was being questioned. This may have been a reminder to me to check if I was using the newly-offensive "he." Or maybe not.

As expertise about plants and animals started to disappear from biology departments in Arts and Sciences, paradoxically it began to reappear in departments in the College of Resource Development. My old Ornithology course started to be taught in Natural Resources Science in Resource Development.

By the late '80s, the distribution of biology faculty in departments and colleges no longer made sense. Also, many of the biology or biology related departments in Resource Development were tiny, and facing extinction due to lack of majors. Discussions began, and a committee formed (LESTF) to look at different ways to stir the pot.

As I looked over this letter again, it was almost eerily prophetic, although it took over two decades for everything to come to pass. The new college that was finally formed in 1998 WAS called the College of Environment and Life Sciences (CELS). My, what a coincidental acronym for a unit that was trying to move away from whole organism biology, and it DID have much more of a practical orientation than Arts and Sciences. One of the sentences in the then contemporary CELS dean's mission statement was "One of the big responsibilities is to be a key component of economic development, to help people achieve their dreams and to maximize their opportunities for success." This seems to be a bit different than the following portion of the contemporary mission statement of Arts and Sciences, "The College promotes students' ethical and intellectual development and capabilities through critical and independent thinking, reading, and communicating." The following table will suggest how different student requirements were for similar majors in the different colleges, like Zoology in A & S, and Animal Science in Resource Development:

College Graduation Requirements (credits)		
	Resource Development	A & S
Fine Arts	0	6
Letters	0	6
Social Sciences	0	6
Natural Sciences	0	6
Math	3	3
Communications	0	6
Foreign Language	0	Intermediate

In the 2000s the new college picked up a very aggressive and ambitious Dean with a molecular biology background (after having a very aggressive and ambitious interim Dean who was also Dean of Oceanography). Initially, there WAS a big difference between the general education curricular requirements of CELS and Arts and Sciences (Arts and Sciences was more demanding), and differences remain, but today the differences between colleges are smaller because the OTHER colleges lowered their own requirements for the reason proposed in the letter—uncommitted students tend to gravitate toward less-demanding programs, and a small department can't survive with only committed students.

One outcome is surprising to me. Other than a fusion of Botany and Zoology into Biological Sciences, most of the old Resource Development departments remain more or less intact, although shrunken, and in some cases, renamed. In the mid '00s the then-new CELS Dean made a serious attempt to have discussions about a new structure for departments (including as an option the elimination of departments), but nothing came from these talks at the time. However, in a practical sense, departments are no longer the functional units of the college. The most significant change was the shift of the awarding of teaching assistantships from departments to the college. TA'ships are now used to reward "productive" faculty who are good rainmakers, and the idea that a particular potential TA would be admitted because he or she had expertise in a required upper division course seems to have gone by the boards.

During my brief sojourn as chair of Biological Sciences in the early '00s, I could hear a great slurping sound, as chairs' prerogatives were gradually sucked up by the college. The days when a chair could shape a department by executive decisions were pretty much over when I finished my term.

In the early part of the '80s, it became clear to the members of the Botany and Zoology Departments (then both still in the College of Arts and Sciences), that the higher university administration *really wanted* there to be a fusion of the two departments, and that hybrid would be in the new College of the Life and Environmental Sciences. The faculty members of the departments concerned had mixed feelings, mostly neutral to negative. It was an unlikely union. The two departments were physically in different buildings on opposite sides of campus, rarely went to each other's seminars, tended not to socialize together, and the Zoology Department was twice as big as Botany. The drive for fusion, as was almost always the case for large-scale changes like this, originated outside the units concerned, and was economic in nature. Similar movements were happening on campuses all over the United States, as resources were stretched, and enrollments increased. I suspect that this story was repeated many times.

Zoology was in good shape. We had hundreds of majors, ran the premed program, and had half a dozen courses with enrollments over 150. Our faculty/student ratio was golden (i.e., each faculty member taught on average very large numbers of students. Therefore our cost/student was low). Botany's optics were not as good. They had very few majors, and only handsfull of students in their upper division courses, thus their cost/student was high. On the other hand, the few faculty members they had tended to be very active researchers, and they had a couple of real rainmakers.

However, as we approached mid-decade, it was apparent that there WOULD be a merger, and no matter how we felt about it, it was going to happen. Nevertheless, I was amazed to see that almost nobody in either department was interested in planning for the merger. Perhaps because I had a life outside the university, I knew that unplanned mergers could be disastrous.

At the time, I was Chairman of the Board of Directors of the South Kingstown Public Housing Authority, where we had a $2 million annual budget, and I supervised $13 million in capital projects. I was also on the board of directors of the volunteer Friends of the Kingston Station that was working with the state of RI to restore the historic Kingston railroad station—$2 million. Being an avid railroad enthusiast, I was well aware of the difficulties railroads had when they merged.

As a result, I circulated a memo about planning for a merger to my colleagues in both departments. I had been prompted to do so when a member of the Botany department came over to our building to do something, and I started schmoozing with him. Talk of merger was much in the air, so out of curiosity, I asked him what committees Botany had. He looked puzzled, and I explained that we had an undergraduate committee, a graduate committee, a finance committee, etc. He said they didn't have any committees; they did everything as a committee of the whole. There was a grad student using the copy machine, and I asked the botanist what his department's policy was about grad students using the copy machine. We had to set limits because the grad students were making copies of their dissertations and eating up thousands of sheets of paper a month. He said they didn't have a policy—they had so few grads that they just let them copy away. I knew we were in for trouble.

It really came to a head at the Christmas party in 1994. The Zoology parties had always been rowdy affairs held in our building. Then, by edict of the campus president, the campus went dry, so we moved the party to my house, which was big enough to comfortably accommodate it.

Now, to appreciate what follows, you have to understand that we had a long-standing custom for our Christmas parties in Zoology, a special kind of Secret Santa. You drew names, and an unknown person would give you a package with a card. At the party, you had to read the card aloud and then open the present in front of the group. Zoologists, by training and history, tend to be a fairly earthy group of people, so the presents were designed to be as bawdy as possible, given heavily to sex toys and the like.

In the interest of getting the members of the two, soon-to-be-joined departments together, my wife and I invited members of both old departments to a joint Christmas party at our house. Whereas the Zoology party had always been after work in the Zoology building on a weekday, that wouldn't work for a joint party, so it was scheduled to start at 8 p.m. on a Saturday night.

Came Saturday, my wife and I were still putting the house together, when at 8:00:00 p.m. there was a knock on the door. It was the Chair of Botany, his wife, and their *two adorable little girls*. Oh my GOD!! Who comes to an eight o'clock Saturday party at eight o'clock? Who brings kids to an Animal House party? Now, you have to understand that the Chair of Botany was one of the smartest, nicest, sweetest guys in the world, but it was instantly evident that the old *Botany* parties must have been very sedate, family-friendly affairs.

Despite the inauspicious start, and our having no idea how to amuse the little girls, the food and wine flowed, and everything was fine until Secret Santa time. Everybody gathered around the fireplace, and the Chair of Botany, his wife, and the little pinafored girls had front row seats on the couch.

Santa gave the first present out to a grad student who worked in invertebrate Zoology. It was beautifully wrapped, and sort of looked about the size and shape of—a Kielbasa. All the Zoologists' faces were frozen in horrified anticipation, as the little girls smiled and looked at the speaker. He pulled the note out of the envelope and started to read. "Dear Jim. Secret Santa knows that you are fascinated by the invertebrate animals. Your specialty is the taxonomy of the group. It is the heart's dream of every invertebrate zoologist to discover, describe, and name a new species. Jim, Secret Santa has found for you a Worm Unknown to Science, and you will have the honor of naming it." I have to give 'ol Jim a lot of credit. He could feel that the Worm Unknown to Science was actually a giant double dildo, so he immediately went into a coughing fit, excused himself, and went to the bathroom. In the meantime, Santa juggled the presents so that the next couple went to botanists. When opened, they were really nice, thoughtful gifts. In the meantime Santa did some fast interviews to see which Zoology presents were suitable for public revelation, ditched the others, and my wife saved the day by suggesting a trivia game, prematurely sending Secret Santa to the showers. I don't think the Botanists ever found out what happened.

Despite my memo, not much happened before the merger took place the following year. The Botany department felt that they had been steamrollered into the affair, and were losing assets in the process. As it turned out *both* Zoology and Botany lost assets—but not to each other. The real winner was the new college. Despite Zoology's efforts to make the Botanists feel like co-equals, resentments lingered for a decade, but seem now to have been pretty much forgotten with the retirement of the old-timers.

Chapterlet 8 · Greenhorn Faculty

1969 was a tumultuous year. Apollo 11 on the moon. Woodstock festival. The Beatles release "Abbey Road." However, after September, I wasn't aware of any of this, because I was getting ready to teach my first megacourse, Biology 2, at the University of Rhode Island, and I had about a week's notice.

Bio 2 was taught in Edwards Auditorium, a beautiful old granite structure built in 1928, essentially like a movie theater for silent films. It had 1,009 seats, divided between a main floor and a balcony. There was a huge movie screen mounted above an elevated stage with a red velvet curtain. A projection booth in the back served when films or slides were displayed. There was an enormous theater pipe organ to accompany films, and behind the stage there were green rooms, presumably to let lecturers prepare themselves for lecture. The only concession to use as a lecture hall was a podium with the university seal, bolted stage left on the stage. A single, inferior quality microphone was fastened to the front of the podium. You may be surprised that I remember these details from 50 years ago. I'm 79 years old and can't remember what I had for breakfast, but I remember that the stairs from the stage to the orchestra pit were on stage left.

For my first lecture, I tried to emulate my hero Richard Eakin, mentioned in an earlier chapter. I typed out my first lecture as a script, but there wasn't time to memorize it, so when the time came I delivered it like a political speech; quickly glance down and memorize a couple of lines, look up to maintain eye contact, then look down when it's time for the next lines.

I'm searching for the correct word to describe this first megalecture of my career. Debacle? No, not strong enough. Calamity? Closer. Cataclysm? Yup, about right. When it was over, I got off the stage with the speed of light, and started to think over alternate careers, like sewer pipe welder.

The next few lectures were a little better, but it didn't take long for me to realize that to be an effective Large Class lecturer, you had to make the students somehow forget that they were in a giant auditorium, and THINK that you were talking to them personally. You couldn't *actually* talk to each of them personally, but terrific large class lecturers could somehow produce that illusion and they did it through a skill that I convinced myself I might learn with some effort. What was that skill?

Stagecraft.

I managed to survive the first semester, and when I taught the same class in the second semester, it was much smaller, only about 600 students, It also was the second time around for the lectures, so they were much better, and gave me a little more free time that I was able to use to try some experiments.

One of the things I almost intuitively knew was that when you talk to someone, their facial expressions are almost as important as their words—sometimes more important. From smiles or frowns we can gauge the importance of spoken words, or their truthfulness. But, how are you going to read the expressions on somebody's face when they're standing 60 feet in front of you? Today, it might be very different (and more challenging). Glued to their electronic devices, face-to-face and eye contact seem to be less important to students.

By this time, I had attracted a small coterie of students in an informal after-class coffee and chat group. During an hour when the auditorium was empty, I grabbed one of the students (not literally, you had to be careful even in those days), and had her stand up on the stage where I normally stood. I also turned on the spotlights I normally used. I sat in one of the back rows. I had her read from the script. Her face was just a tiny pink oval with a couple of dots on it. I couldn't see eyebrows raised, smile—nothing. All her facial features were washed out. If I turned off the spotlight, her face was too dark to see features. That convinced me that if I was going to significantly improve as a large class lecturer, I'd have to get some professional instruction—from the theater department.

I asked around and found the costume and makeup teacher, whose name was Joy Spanabel. I explained my problem, and asked if she had any suggestions. She seemed a little surprised, and said no large-class lecturer had ever asked her about this issue before, but she thought it would address the communication question. She would show me how to do it, but I'd have to buy a stage makeup kit first.

This was before internet shopping, and I was totally clueless about what to order, where to order it, and how much it would cost. I blanched when I found out how much I was going to have to pay for such a kit. I just looked up a comparable one, and pro-grade kits run about $250 now.[2]

Feelings about men who wear makeup were a little different then than they are now, so I didn't mention my experiment to many people. In practice,

---

[2] I go into more detail in my book, Heppner, F. (2007), *Teaching the Large College Class*, San Francisco, CA: Jossey-Bass.

because I wasn't trying to make up like the Phantom of the Opera or anything like that, I could set up in about 15 minutes, and clean up in 5. I lied a little bit and told the students in the class that I couldn't see them immediately after class because I had a little digestive problem I had to address, but I would be happy to meet them in the front of the auditorium a few minutes after the lecture was over. After a couple of years, when I had a lot more confidence, I told the class what I was doing to make communication better in lecture, and somewhat surprisingly to me, nobody seemed to be bothered—by this time I was starting to demonstrate other eccentricities, and apparently they figured it was part of the package.

I mentioned in a previous chapter that I started doing a version of multimedia before it even had a name. The auditorium had a very wide, CinemaScope-type projection screen, and I could easily project the images from two slide projectors side-by-side at the same time. Preparing slides with complex images was MUCH more difficult than today, but that's why we had a departmental artist. I started using music before lectures to get the students used to starting on time, but after while, it became kind of fun to develop slide shows that also had music. Like Eakin, I tried to have a knock 'em dead Last Lecture, but instead of a live talk, it gradually morphed into a multiple slide projector program. And instead of Eakin's inspiring lecture (which I was later to emulate), it gave me a chance to exercise a little black humor. This was the era of split-screen in the movies, like *Grand Prix*, and *Carrie*, and I figured if two slide projectors were good, nine projectors would be even better. There were about six "stories" in the final product. One was about what happened to a student who cheated. After thinking he had gotten away with it, a garbage truck accidentally dumped its load in his little British sports car while he was in it. My favorite was a sketch about how we graded their exams—and in it we confirmed their worst suspicions. Here's how it went:

When they took their exams, they entered their answers on an IBM punch card, which we collected at the end of the exam. The sketch started in the auditorium, with the students sweating over answers, and the proctors standing with stony expressions on their faces, arms folded like prison guards. To make the audience feel at ease, the background music was Mozart's Requiem In D Minor, K. 626:3. Sequentia:Dies Irae, which is, of course, the Mass for the Dead.

At the end of the exam, the TA's collected the answer cards and put them in a big box. We all then marched, expressionless, across campus to my lab, which was in an underground building. We went downstairs, and gathered in front of my office door. When I opened the door, they saw a darkened room with a long black lab table in the center, with three chairs on either side, and one at the head. A hangman's noose dangled over the center of the table. At each side seating spot, there was an empty beaker, and at the head there was a candle burning in a holder attached to a skull, and a large flask that apparently contained blood. There was a green gradebook next to the flask.

The head TA put the box at the head of the table, and we all took seats. I sat at the head, next to the exams. I rose, and poured some "blood" into each beaker. On signal, we all drained our beakers. We immediately clutched our throats in agony, and smoke filled the room, blocking out our images. When it cleared, the TA's had been transformed into zombies and ghouls, and I was Count Dracula. The camera shifted to the open gradebook, with all the students' (fictional) names listed in alphabetical order. I picked out the first card in the stack, which had been alphabetized. I stuck the end of the card in the candle flame, it immediately caught fire, and the smoke that arose formed the letter "F." All the zombies clapped their hands in delight, and the grade was entered in the book. There then followed several more card burnings, all to the same effect, and then the camera went back to the gradebook, whose first page was filled. All "F's."

Slide from Last Lecture in Bio 2, showing how grade cards are corrected.

The screen faded to black, and then a title appeared. It said, "Don't let this happen to you; Study More." Fade to black again. I should add that the students were laughing all through the presentation.

In many fields, including mine, research was in the early stages, and early stage research is usually less expensive than later stage, where equipment becomes more complicated (and expensive). When I was an experimental biologist in the early days, thanks to shop knowledge I picked up as a kid I was able to make most of my own apparatus, out of junk and war surplus. So I didn't need grants, which gave me a huge amount of time. Later investigators needed more precise (expensive) store-bought equipment.

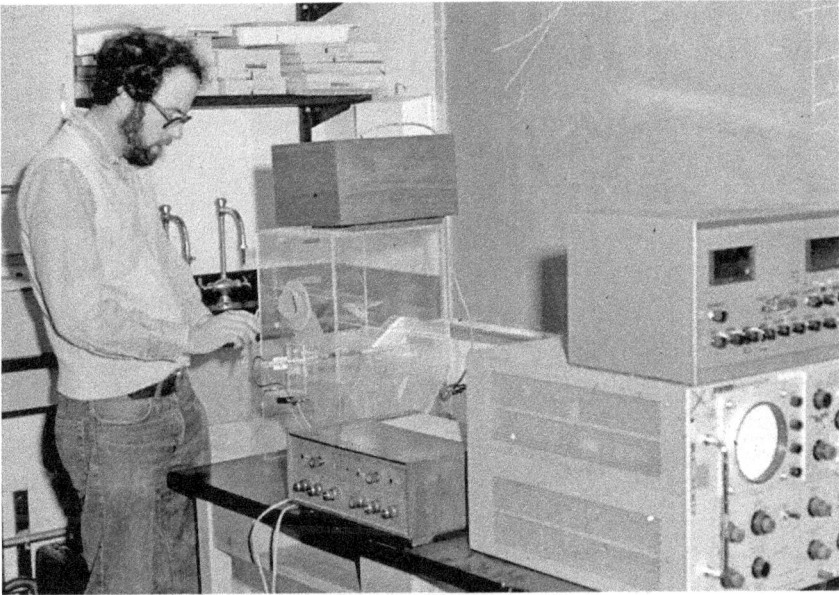

Equipment to test reaction times in birds. All the equipment was either home made (chamber and control panel), war surplus (oscilloscope), or borrowed from home (stereo speakers). The paper came out in 1977, and was most recently cited in 2020.

As I look back on this, several things come to mind. First, I had time to do it. Even though I had what today would be considered a heavy teaching load, and an active research lab, my bureaucratic busywork load was minimal, and I was under no pressure to get grants. That is very different today. Also, I think there was more eccentricity in the professorate. There were at least two other profs in my department who were as weird as I was, and about a half dozen others to a lesser degree. I'd like to tell you about one of them, who was a good friend, now alas working in the Great Lab in the Sky.

His name was Bob Shoop, and he studied reptiles and amphibians in the field. He was one rank ahead of me when I came to URI. He was a pilot and taught me how to fly in his old 1956 Cessna 172 single engine plane. He kept the plane at a short, very short, private runway near campus. The runway was 1,700 feet long, and the plane needed 1,575 feet to take off—but a high voltage powerline ran across the runway at one end, and there was a hill at the other end. So you got it right, or you got dead. On the other hand, learning on a runway like that was a confidence builder. If you could land on that, you could land on anything.

He did most of his research in the South, on Cumberland Island, Georgia, where he had a cabin. No electricity, no running water, and he would stay there for three months at a time during summer. There were rattlesnakes all over, and sometimes one would say howdy in the privy.

Back at URI, before the campus went dry, he would have SOB's (seminars over beer) on Friday afternoons after classes. Most of the participants were grad student field biologists, and they were invited to give presentations about their research trips. This was good practice for them when it came time for hiring seminars.

At one point, he introduced a contest called "mystery meat." He would bring in samples of meat, often road kill, that he would slow-cook up. Students were supposed to identify the animal by the characteristics of the cooked meat—after all, they all wanted to be Zoologists, and Zoologists should be able to identify animals, even by their pieces.

For some animals, it was fairly easy. Deer were the most common roadkills in our area, but raccoons and possums were also fairly easily identified by taste. One day he brought something in that nobody could identify. He then came over and started razzing me. I was a *bright* guy and should be able to figure it out. How come I was being so *quiet* about it? Finally he said, "Will make you very *smart!*" I reacted in mock horror, and said, "No! Not Woodsy the Owl!" Alas, that's what it was. Somehow a barn owl got confused, and flew right into the radiator of his truck. Have to say, Woodsy, even after three hours of slow roasting, was pretty tough.

Bob Shoop reaching into a bag to pull out the
Mystery Snake.

Chapter 21
Out of the Ashes

This story has a happy ending, but it could just as easily have gone the other way, and my academic career would have been over in 1984. That it didn't was due more to good luck than effort on my part. The tale does illustrate how creeping bureaucratization has gradually affected every part of college life.

I started my career as an experimental biologist. I alternated between field and lab studies on birds right from the start in 1962. By the late '70s–early '80s I had a small bird colony established in the then-new Biological Sciences Center (BISC) building. The birds were housed in rooms that had specifically been designed to accommodate experimental animals. My grad students and I had cranked out a number of studies that found their way into journals like *Nature* and when the studies were complete, the birdies (English Sparrows, normally considered a pest species like rats, and unprotected by law) were released back to the wild from whence they came. Once again they would have the opportunity to dodge cats, and scrounge their own food. Life was good. I got papers, and the birds got "three hots and a cot" for a couple of months (if you're not familiar with this useful expression, look it up).

In 1981–1982, I went to the Philippines for a year on a Fulbright sabbatical. On my return, I got a rather unpleasant surprise. I was informed that URI was shutting down all experimental animal facilities in BISC, because the rooms didn't meet the then-new ventilation standards for experimental animal quarters established by the National Institutes of Health. These regs had been introduced in 1979, but took a couple of years to become operational. At the time, there were only two faculty members who kept animals in BISC; myself and a guy who worked on ferrets. The university was building a new animal facility off campus, but during my sojourn in the jungle, I didn't hear about it, and as a result, didn't apply for space. As a result, all space in the new facility was already committed by my return.

In my files were dozens of letters to every administrator I could think of on campus who might be able to help. It was my worst bureaucratic nightmare come true. I discovered that the ventilation standards for lab mice were higher than for humans. There was no way to economically upgrade the facility in BISC. The regulations had been written for mammals like mice, and birds were not specifically mentioned in a lot of the regs and were thus subject to local (and variable) contradictory interpretation. The official channels at URI were sympathetic, but understandably, they were more interested in protecting funded research than my shoestring self-funded efforts. The other guy with animals in BISC got fed up and moved himself and his ferrets to the University of Montana in 1983, so I was the surviving homeless lab rat.

Finally, on January 23, 1984, I received the death warrant. The URI Central Laboratory Animal Facilities Committee decided that much as it would like to help, it couldn't accommodate my birds. The last sentence of the letter was wonderful. "Best of luck with your research program."

Now what? In looking over my old resume, it looks like I just floated for a couple of years. Had I been younger, that would have been the end of my career. But I was already a Full Professor, and had the luxury of time to find something else. I switched over to writing texts, and articles about teaching. I also started dabbling again with field observations of birds (even that kind of research later came under the animal welfare regulations too, as mentioned previously). I eventually had to apply for permission from the Animal Welfare Committee to watch robins in my back yard for scientific purposes, although I could still watch them for pleasure without a permit.

In 1985, I bought my first personal computer, a far-ahead-of-its-time job called an Amiga. Believe it or not, it had a flight simulator that ran on 512K of memory. One of the bundled demonstration programs was something called "The Game of Life," which had originally been developed for mainframe computers in the early '70s by a man named John Conway. It wasn't really a game, but a demonstration of a computer concept called a "cellular automaton." Briefly, you placed "dots" on the screen in any pattern you wanted. You then made a "move" and the dots persisted or disappeared depending on their relationship to other dots. You could make a complex pattern of dots morph into another pattern because each dot followed a set of simple rules: (http://www.conwaylife.com/).

I was playing with it one day, and all of a sudden, it occurred to me that these dots could be arranged in patterns that looked like a flock of pigeons. One of the big issues of the day was: do pigeon flocks have leaders, or is there some other, unknown mechanism that produced the synchrony when they made synchronous turns? So I played with the idea for a while, and came up with the thought that if you had the right set of rules, you could simulate a turning and wheeling bird flock on a computer, and maybe real birds had a similar set of simple rules that they used to produce synchronous turns.

In 1987, I gave a paper on the idea at a bird meeting in San Francisco. Bird people were not computer people in those days, and since I couldn't provide an actual demonstration, nobody knew what I was talking about, so it didn't exactly create a sensation. On my return, however, through mutual friends I met a brilliant applied mathematician named Ulf Grenander at Brown. He was fascinated by the idea, and for the next year or so he taught me computers and I taught him birds. We developed an actual simulation and presented it at the American Association of Sciences meeting in New Orleans in 1990. It got picked up by the national press, and I had the heady experience of giving interviews for a few weeks.

That started me on the *next* 20 years of my research life, and I'm convinced I went much further than I would have if I had stayed on with birds in the lab. So, thanks to the bureaucrats at NIH, and the animal rights, ah, *folks*, for shutting me down at just the right time. Alas, there were other scientists, some of whom I knew, who never hurt an animal in their lives, who had to leave research completely. Luck of the draw.

Chapter 22
Budget—It's Always the Damned Budget

I'm still on a couple of URI faculty e-lists. Recently, I received a copy of the latest "Academic Strategy Partner's Report" coming out of the university Provost's office. The first one I could find came out in 2013. The graphics in the newer one are a little snazzier, but both were given to ambitious sound bites: "Overarching Emphasis: Innovation with Impact. Exciting and relevant collaborations deeply rooted in **innovation** [*sic*] that push the frontiers of learning, discovery, and problem solving."

Great ideas, Boss, but how do you propose we do this with 20% more students, but 10% more income? I'm not really sure who the audience is for whom these documents are intended, but I suspect they don't live in the university's zip code. Not that I'm unsympathetic with the plight of the current folks in the administration building who are trying to keep URI going and improving, but their struggle is nothing new. One of the most common topics of in-house correspondence I found dated between 1980–1998 was how dire the budget situation was, and what awful kinds of things would result if a cash injection didn't immediately follow.

The first was a letter from me to the Chair of Zoology in 1980, suggesting that with the recent 25% cut in my lab class budget, I could not in good conscience offer a competitive laboratory experience for the students enrolled in my big first-year class, therefore with his permission I was going to close 25% of my lab sections. Somewhat ungrammatically, I suggested that "Bluntly, it is either more money or less students." This letter was forwarded to the Dean with the Chair's approval.

I don't have a recollection of ever actually shutting sections down after students had already enrolled, so I have a feeling that somehow, from somewhere, my lab supplies budget was increased. What MAY be different today is my suspicion that if an adjunct faculty member now made the same promise/threat, there would be a new adjunct found whose standards of "quality" might be somewhat more realistic for the times.

When I came to URI in 1969, budget wasn't the big issue in campus politics. The university was ambitious and expanding, and the new hires all had the expectation that things were only going to be bigger and better. The turnaround was gradual and I believe started in the late 1970s. How come? Here I'm entering the ranks of the speculators, but I suspect that it had something to do with the observation my old post-doc advisor made before I took the job. He said that Rhode Island was a blue-collar state, and felt neither the need nor the desire for a major, state-supported university.

However, during the '60s, URI, like many other second- and third-tier research universities around the country, was sharing in the bonanza of federal science and engineering funds made available during and immediately after the space race. John Knauss, Dean of Oceanography was extremely adapt at securing defense related oceanographic money, and President Werner Baum, who came in '68 with a science background, continued the building boom of the '60s. Baum left for greener pastures in 1973, and was replaced by Frank Newman, whose background was essentially in politics and the politics of education. It was well into Newman's tenure that the real budget crunches started.

During the '70s, URI had a number of PR disasters and near-disasters, many involving the effect on the surrounding community of URI's expansion, and I suspect that as the decade began to come to a close, the public and the legislature began to realize that it was going to be far more costly to develop URI into a national-class university than they anticipated in the '60s, and the old saw that you have to spend money to make money was true with a vengeance—but there was less certainty now that a huge investment would pay off. I believe that's why the relative state contribution to total expenses tapered off in the late '70s.

But the owner of Sal's Pizza's kid still had to go to school to become an accountant, so URI continued to receive enough state funds to fulfill that function, but if URI wanted to go beyond that, the legislative feeling appeared to be that it bloody well was going to have to raise the money itself. I think this is why, as I demonstrated earlier, we began to see "revised standards of academic excellence" for out-of-state students, and increased pressure on faculty to get grants.

Could we have gone a different way at the time? I really don't think so. All the New England state universities and many others around the country were experiencing the same phenomenon, with much the same results. In its 2019 budget, the University of Vermont received 12% of its revenue from the state, 6% from in-state tuition, and 51% from out-of-state tuition. Even in the lofty University of California, the state only provides 11% of the operating budget. Only if we had made the radical change to become more specialized, and concentrate only on areas where we could be locally or regionally

122

competitive might there have been a difference, but that would have been (and I think still is) politically challenging on URI's or any campus. After all, *everybody* has dreams of glory, and it would be unlikely at best for a campus administration to say something like, "Colleagues, we don't have the resources to enable all departments to have a shot at the brass ring, so after careful study and the report of our consultants, we've decided to quadruple the budget of our Department of New England Cryptozoology and give them five new tenure-track positions, while making the Departments of Chemistry, English, and Psychology into service departments to cut their expenses. Their only new hires will be adjuncts. Those departments would never be able to compete on a national basis anyway."

Chapter 23
The Good Leader

When I was a teenager in the 1950s, I loved high school ROTC. It was a very different climate—the Korean War had just ended, and almost everyone's dad had served in WWII, or didn't come back from it. There was very little anti-military feeling about in the land.

High school ROTC at the time was a very odd institution. There were two kinds of kids who joined. First, non-athletic nerds like me who took it as a way to avoid gym. Then, troublemakers who had been *kicked out* of gym for being discipline problems. So there was the strange situation where kids who looked like the cast of Big Bang Theory had to give and enforce *orders* to a World Wrestling Entertainment tag-team. It was wonderful preparation for leadership in a university.

We were forced to memorize a little maxim called "The Good Leader." It made a powerful impression on me, and guided my life in most areas outside the university. I remember it to this day, but I couldn't find it on Google, so I don't know where it came from.

The Good Leader
"The Good Leader ensures that his men have food before he eats. The Good Leader rests only after his men find sleep. The Good Leader only comes in from the storm after his men find shelter. If he do these things, his men will follow him to the gates of Hell."

The buzz phrase that described this was "Leadership by Example." It served me well as a volunteer search-and-rescue pilot in the Air Force Auxiliary, and the various civic groups where I had a leadership role. As I later discovered, it presented certain difficulties at a university.

By the beginning of the 21st century, the Department of Biological Sciences was in deep trouble. Esprit d'corps was non-existent. The merger between Botany and Zoology hadn't really worked. Faculty, especially the younger ones, were under tremendous pressure to become grant-getting rainmakers above all else. But what was most ominous was that we were RICH in assets that were coveted almost everywhere on campus. We became a fat, juicy target for dismemberment or absorption.

Here's why.

We had a tremendous number of high-enrollment first and second year lab courses. Everybody on the faculty complained about them, tried to get out of teaching them, and I was one of only two faculty members who really like to teach them, BUT—they required dozens of teaching assistants. We needed so many that every grad student admitted to the department was offered a TA'ship. We even offered TA'ships to grad students in other departments. So other biology-related departments were starving for TA'ships, but we were giving them away.

These big courses were also, literally, cash cows. Students' lab fees came direct and intact to the department that offered the course the students were taking. At the time, they were about $50 a course, and the department picked up almost $100,000 (about $200,000 in 2019 dollars) a year. However, the actual lab costs per individual student for the big courses were typically about $10 a head. So the big courses lavishly subsidized the much smaller upper division courses. You need a $15,000 spectroscope for your 12 students in Biology of the Cockroach? No problem, Jack. And, by a *strange coincidence,* the equipment used in the upper division teaching labs could in many cases be used for the professor's personal research, or as seed money for grant proposals.

The situation was *exactly* as described in Danny DeVito's 1980s movie "Other People's Money." The department was ripe to be absorbed by a larger unit which could strip it of its assets, or split it apart and redistribute its assets to other departments. And that is exactly what happened. We were worth more dead than alive.

In 2002, our old Chair had resigned, and we were chairless. Nobody wanted the job because it was personally costly in terms of professional development, unless you had plans to move into administration, which nobody did. Several of my colleagues knew that I had leadership experience outside the university, and a history of volunteerism. I was persuaded to throw my hat in the lonely ring.

However, I didn't want to do it unless people knew what they were buying. So, I prepared a document, a manifesto, really, which was distributed to the department and the college Dean. As I looked it over now, I was even at that time naively trying to plant the seeds of "Leadership by Example."

At the appropriate time, the department voted me in as chair. I took this to mean that they were aware of the direction I wanted to take, and approved of it. Eh, wrong! Almost none of the policies I advocated were eventually adopted, but as it turned out, I was a pretty good prognosticator. Most of my dire predictions came true. We WERE absorbed, and many of our assets were stripped away. Now, TA'ships for grad students to assist in our courses are not awarded by the department but given as rewards to "productive" faculty in the college, regardless of department.

As soon as I took office, I proceeded to try to put "Leadership by Example" into place. I knew that the handwriting was on the wall that faculty, even active researchers, would sooner or later have to deal with increased undergraduate teaching. The chair was normally relieved of half his/her teaching load. I kept my normal assignment, which was already the heaviest in the department (by my choice). I figured the other faculty would see this, and say something like, "If he's going to do that, well, I can do it too."

Well, I made a real mistake here, and it's my fault—I just didn't see it coming. Academia does not have the same culture as the military, and we do not have either a strongly hierarchical tradition, or one of rewarding sacrifice for the benefit of the group. So instead of being inspired by my voluntary heavy teaching load, the almost universal response was, "Thank God Frank still teaches that stupid course. Now *I* won't have to do it, and can concentrate on my important research." That sounds sort of catty, but I don't mean it that way. We *are* trained and rewarded to believe that our individual research *is* important, and *that* is how we make our major contribution to society.

I served one term as Chair. It wasn't a great experience for either me or the department. I had to preside as the department changed colleges, an action that was almost universally unpopular, as we could see that our resources were being gobbled up by the new structure. For example, undergraduate lab fees used to come to the department. Afterwards they went to the college. Unfunded research, no matter how good or widely recognized, was not considered in allocation of resources, or teaching assignments. Now, it appears that the only knowledge that is worth searching for is that which brings outside funding. Too bad.

Chapterlet 9 · Extracurricular Activity

When I came to Rhode Island in 1969, I was immediately struck by the difference in world view I grew up with in San Francisco, and the Yankee perspective of the small town where I first decided to live, the village of Wickford, about 12 miles north of URI. I had done various sorts of volunteer work all the way back to high school, so once things squared away on campus, I decided to volunteer to do something in town. But what to do?

My father had passed away in 1967, and I was the executor of his estate, responsible for taking care of my mother back home. The money from his estate had to be invested, and I saw right away that there was an active real estate market in R.I., and decided to give it a whack by rehabbing low income rental units. My adventures, and that's what they were, are outlined in a book I recently wrote.

Because of this real estate experience, I thought maybe I could serve on something exciting, like the Zoning Board, so I went down to the Town Hall and volunteered my services. Surprisingly, months went by before I got a call from the Town Clerk. I had been appointed to a vacant seat on the Conservation Commission and I had to go to the next meeting in a couple of weeks to have my appointment confirmed.

Wanting to make a good impression, I arrived early at the Town Hall. They had already started the meeting so I was late. Swell. There was one seat vacant at the conference table, so I took it and nodded, pleasantly I hoped, to the other members. The Chairman introduced himself, then gave the following little speech, which I have tried to reproduce phonetically, in the dialect of a Swamp Yankee, or "Swampah," as the long-time residents of southern Rhode Island are known.

"Thank you fer comin', Mistah' Heppnah. Befo' we staht, I want t' let you know that most of ouh' families have been heah' fo' a while. Ah'm fifth generation, Bob over theah, his family has been heah since the place was called Updike's Newtowne, 'bout 1707, and the otha' three, thea' families have been heah' since the eighteen hundreds. So theah's no way you could really undahstand all tha' ins and outs of properteh' use round heah.' But with all these new environmental things comin' down from the state, we figgered we'd be bettah' off with a scientist on the boad,' and we recon' that's what you are from down URI. So we'll really appreciate what ya' can tell us 'bout that, but fo' all the rest, you can just make yaself' comf' table, 'cause we won't need ya' fo' anythin' else."

Under normal circumstances, I would have told him to bugger off and find a dark place for his board, but I looked at it as a cultural experiment, and after a couple of months of keeping my yap shut, and speaking only when spoken to, I discovered something remarkable. These folks were just as friendly and nice as could be! But in their daily lives they never ran into anybody who wasn't a swampah,' because they rarely left South County, and just didn't know how to talk to a strangah.' After that, I was sorry to leave Wickford when I moved closer to the university in 1976, although the distinctive qualities of the Swamp Yankees have pretty much disappeared by now.

I then started a series of further real estate ventures that established my housing cred, and was eventually asked to volunteer for the South Kingstown Public Housing Authority Board of Directors. After about 5 years, I was voted in to serve as Chairman of the Board (has a nice ring, doesn't it? Too bad it didn't come with a salary).

There had recently been some huge scandals in Washington involving the parent organization of the local authority, Housing and Urban Development. So I thought it prudent as one of my first tasks on the job to give a little pep talk to the paid employees, so I gathered them one afternoon—

"Thank you for coming. I just wanted to let you know how much the Board appreciates your services, But I want to make you aware of something you probably know, but just in case. We are a public agency, and as a result, all our financial records are open to the public. Any reporter can come down to look at our books. And we have to let them see them. That means that we need to be spotless in all our business with the community; no favors to any of our friends or relatives we might do business with."

I didn't see any looks of alarm, so I thanked them and let them go. Over the next couple of weeks, though, I looked over our books myself to get the lay of the land. One thing immediately jumped out. In addition to our project housing, we also administered small apartments in the community to meet our overflow. They had to meet our standard of "decent, safe, and sanitary." Typically, they were 3–15 units, and according to our rules, we were supposed to distribute our clients evenly through all the owners.

However, there was one 12-unit place that we always kept filled, regardless of the number of vacancies in other units. That attracted my attention. So I looked up who the owner was. He was the brother-in-law of the clerk who assigned new tenants to the units. Well, that more or less explained it. So I called the clerk in for a little talk.

I told her what I'd found, and said that she would have to stop immediately, and distribute evenly from now on. She immediately burst into tears. A bit surprised at the nature of her reaction, I asked her what was wrong. Between sobs, she said, "My family will kill me," she cried, "they've always depended on me!"

That introduced me to the downside of living in a small, closely related community, which Rhode Island was at the time. I realized the difficulty to near impossibility of being able to significantly change things as an outsider, when I lived in the same community, so after I got things more-or-less in order, I resigned a few years later. Ten years was long enough.

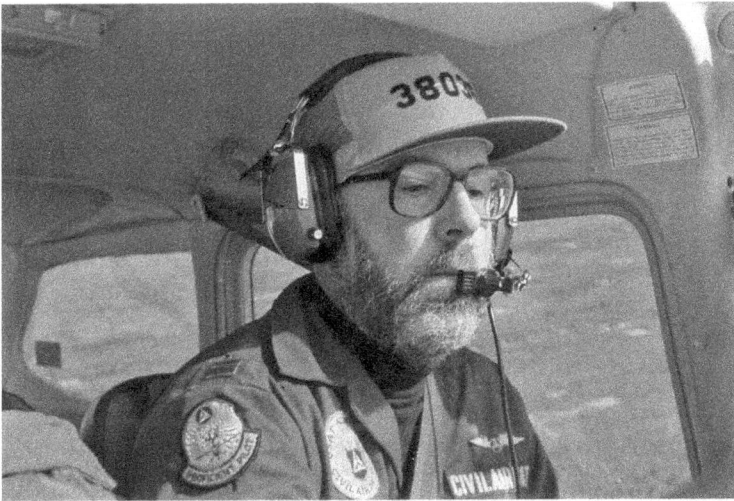

For many years, I served as a volunteer pilot for the Civil Air Patrol.

I also got involved with national volunteer activities. Having gotten a pilot's license in 1977, I joined the Civil Air Patrol and spent many enjoyable (and sometimes terrifying) years as a search and rescue pilot.

The final example of community activity I'll share has a far more positive story but illustrates the difficulty of achieving things through a volunteer/ government partnership. Can be done but requires a LOT of patience.

I arrived in RI by train in 1969. The Kingston train station was an historic structure built in 1875 and was one of the oldest still-standing train stations in the country. It was, however, in dreadful shape—hadn't been painted in 25 years, broken windows, etc. Not an appealing gateway to either the university or the resort areas beyond.

This situation persisted until two members of the URI community, Barbara Dirlam, a faculty wife, and the Rev. John Hall put out a call for volunteers to join a new organization to see what could be done to get the old girl in shape again. In 1972, they formed the Friends of the Kingston Station, mostly populated by URI folks; faculty and staff. In 1974, after endless battles with railroad bureaucracy, the Friends received permission to rehab the building. During a one week period, over 180 volunteers crawled over the station top to bottom, and when they were finished, the station was unrecognizable. The group kept together for a couple of years to work on the interior, then in 1977 disbanded, their work completed.

Fast forward to 1990. Neither Rhode Island nor Amtrak had invested even a fraction of the money an old wooden structure like the station required, so the station was again in poor shape. So the Friends were revived. This time the situation was very different. Due to union regulations, and insurance costs, a volunteer restoration effort was no longer possible. Instead, government money would have to be found and formal bids solicited.

So the Friends adapted to the times. With the aid of Sen Claiborne Pell, they went to endless meetings, wrote hundreds of letters, testified before committees, traveled to Washington, and spent thousands of volunteer hours. Most of the volunteers were still part of the URI community (it should be noted that many of them were also active volunteers on campus, plus being productive in research and teaching).

The result? In 1998, there was a grand celebration that marked the reopening of the station, after an expenditure of about 3 million dollars. Over the next few years patronage at the station quadrupled, and the initial rehab investment was quickly recovered. Today, about 160,000 passengers a year arrive or depart from the station, and it is now the public transportation gateway to southern Rhode Island, and a huge factor in attracting students from the New Haven-Philadelphia area to URI.

I retired from URI 10 years ago, and many of the original faculty members of the Friends are still active. We don't see new members of the faculty joining the Friends, though. They don't have time.

Chapter 24
The Mouse and the Elephant

Once upon a time, a mouse and his family lived in the tent of a circus elephant. Mice and elephants eat the same things, but of course nobody fed the mouse. Instead, he had to dash between the legs of the elephant at feeding time, picking up scraps that had been cast off by the elephant, who was a messy eater, from the feeding trough. The mouse fed his family well, there was only moderate danger, and this situation could have gone on for generations.

However, the mouse was prideful, and the indignity of being essentially a scavenger eventually rankled him. So one day, he climbed up to the edge of the trough, whistled, and called out loudly, "Hey, Jumbo!"

The elephant turned around, ambled over to the trough, and balefully looked down at the mouse.

The mouse said, "Listen, nothing against you, but it's not right that every day you get more food than you can use, but I have to hustle like a bastard to pick up the stuff that falls out of your mouth. It's only fair that from now on, when you get fed, what would it hurt you to push just a little bit over the edge of the trough where I can get it without having to worry about getting stepped on?"

The elephant glared at him for a couple of seconds, then with a lightning blow of his trunk, crushed the mouse like a bug.

Moral of the Story: Mice shouldn't challenge elephants.

If you got this far, you might wonder if I have any conclusions about the past and future of second- and third-tier universities like URI after four decades of reasonably close observation of the place and the people, and with respect to that, I do.

URI has never come to grips with the fact that it is a mouse, not unlike many other nearby mice, surrounded by very large elephants. There are over 250 colleges and universities in New England, including Harvard, MIT, Northeastern, and Boston University—all of which compete with URI in some areas. Mice can make a very nice living as long as they realize that they're mice. However, URI, like many other similar universities, aspires to be an elephant, and every time it grows visible enough in some area to be a challenge to the REAL elephants, they can squash it like a bug.

Time and time again, we have seen that a new administration has started down directions that are trendy, pressworthy, and have a lot of money floating around, only to eventually see that investment end up in the wastewater processing facility. Why is this?

The problem seems to be that the ambitious newcomer (or an ambitious old-timer) identifies a new scholarly area that is currently in early stages of development, has a lot of buzz, and seems to have a ready supply of capital available. So a Center for Research in Lady Gaga Studies is established, possibly with an undergraduate minor within the Department of Outrageous Pop Stars. A couple of new high-visibility faculty are hired, ideally bringing some grants with them, and some courses are established. The Center does well, attracts a lot of publicity, and grows. Eventually NYU hears about it, and is embarrassed because Lady Gaga spent a year there, and they haven't properly recognized her. So they establish their OWN Lady Gaga Studies program, and with their much greater resources, hire away all of URI's Lady Gaga faculty stars.

Does this really happen? I can recall two specific examples at URI. I'll not mention exactly what they were here, because I don't want to embarrass the survivors. One was, let's call it, the Clam Container Program. It was started by a local family that sold clams, and they wanted to both make a contribution, and get a little good publicity for themselves to counterbalance a recent local scandal. They provided enough funds to hire a director, equip a lab, and hire maybe four research faculty and technicians. The university gave a lot of publicity to the program and remodeled a lab but provided no line item funds.

The distinguished clam container researchers did outstanding work over the next couple of years, even though no more family money was forthcoming. Soon, the program caught the attention of the Clam Canning Institute in Aberdeen, Washington. They made a blanket offer to the director and staff, and they left without a look backwards. What is left of URI's Clam Container Program? A search through URI's website finds only one mention. Under "Film Events for Today's Date" it lists Clam Container Program—None. Clearly, the Clam Container Program went down the Memory Hole.

The second program was larger, but suffered the same fate. The university made a sizeable investment in a technology in which URI had no natural advantages, and the staff were eventually hired away by institutions in what was the Silicon Valley of the field.

Okay, so does this mean that an institution of the size and character of URI can't have aspirations of excellence? Absolutely not, but it can't be excellent in all areas. It just doesn't have the resources. Places like URI need to focus on things where they have a natural advantage where it would be difficult for another school in the same "league" to compete. What about other areas at the second-tier school where there isn't an intrinsic advantage? Well, sorry to say, they have to be content with adequate. In university politics this will be hard to do, but the striving for excellence in all areas has been tried for almost half a century, and it just doesn't work.

The State of Rhode Island has the same problem, and has often failed in a similar way. Instead of capitalizing on natural advantages, it has tried to develop things that are politically expedient, and has mostly flopped, making it even harder to develop those things where the state DOES have a fighting chance for prominence.

So, for example, what are URI's natural advantages? Most depend on location. As the Realtors say, "There are three things that matter in property: location, location, and location." If you're in a lousy location, not much you can do about it except move. If you're in a good location, you need to capitalize on it. This is true for colleges as well as houses.

Only 40% of American states have a coastline, and only a tiny fraction of the land area of those states faces the sea. URI is less than 10 miles from both ocean and estuary. Thus, it has not thousands of college competitors in studies on ocean and coast, but dozens, and in those fields of endeavor could compete on an equal basis. There are not a lot of Oceanography programs in Kansas. URI HAS done a pretty good job of this, but I've never had the feeling that administrations over the years have really realized what an asset our marine location is. Plus, we have a couple of examples of blown opportunities.

About 25 years ago, URI started talking about "Marine Biotechnology." Now, this is a pretty specialized area (but one in which URI could have achieved international dominance). Instead, it scrapped the focus and went into "Biotechnology" in general, which put it in direct competition with institutions with many times its resources. My prediction is that if some segment of the present workers at URI in this area develop prominence, they will sooner or later be gobbled up by someplace with much deeper pockets than URI's. This has happened over and over—URI prepared the soil, it bought the tractor, it planted the seeds, then somebody else harvested the corn.

So the motto should have been, "If it's marine; we OWN it!" Does this mean URI and similar institutions will have to downplay or neglect other areas where there are ambitious people on campus? Absolutely.

The second location-related advantage is that URI is in one of the very few places in the United States that has such a wide variety of natural habitats in close proximity. Within an hour's drive, you have coastal, estuary, riverine, lacustrine, suburban, urban, agricultural, forest, abandoned field, etc. etc. About the only things RI doesn't have are montane, and desert. For both teaching and research, the proximity of so many different habitats and their interfaces is an enormous advantage, difficult to duplicate elsewhere. URI does have a 2,300 acre field campus ideally located to capitalize on these research opportunities, but it has never been developed the way it could. Ironically, with the Covid economic crisis, URI has announced plans to shut this campus.

The third area has to do with the very basis for Rhode Island's continued existence as an independent entity. The reason we are still here as the state of Rhode Island, and not as part of southern Massachusetts, is because RI is a major stop on the trade route from Boston to New York, and Narragansett Bay is the last US all-year harbor north of New York harbor. Rhode Island was built not on manufacturing, but trade, and the transshipment of goods and people from one mode of transportation to another. There are not that many relatively small and manageable geographic areas where you have ocean shipping, and relatively uncongested rail, air, and highway shipping in close proximity.

So where could URI fit into this? It could become the national center for intermodal transportation research. The REAL problems in transportation occur where modes of transportation intersect. It's great that you can take a commuter train to Providence, but what do you do when you get off the train? Is the present way containers from ships destined to railcars are unloaded at the port of Quonset REALLY the best way to do it? The research done at URI could be tested (conveniently) in the natural laboratory provided by Quonset, the former naval air station that is now a transshipment center. This kind of stuff COULD be done at New York or Philadelphia, but those areas are so congested and expensive, that RI could compete effectively.

If you're small, go with your strengths, and write off your weaknesses. As a New England state university, no matter what URI administration does, it'll always have a big input of instate students who will come to URI no matter what, and RI beaches will provide an eternal draw for affluent out-of-state students with modest academic qualifications who could give a damn about Biotechnology, so there is an inherent undergraduate draw that would be difficult to duplicate elsewhere, and can provide core income. Many other institutions of the size and prominence of URI have similar local advantages that could be developed.

So, ironically, the less globally ambitious URI is, the more likely it is to be successful, and I believe the same is true for similar colleges and universities.

Chapter 25
So, Does the Bureaucracy Always Win?

This question gave me a good deal of pause. If this were a scholarly book, rather than a memoir, I suspect that the answer might be different, but fair warning, my conclusions are based on personal experiences at a single institution.

When I was a kid in the '50s I read *The Caine Mutiny*, by Herman Wouk. It was an epic novel about the Navy in World War II. The slimiest character was Lt. Keefer, an intellectual writer who, being a free spirit, hated everything about the Navy and its stifling bureaucracy.

At one point, Keefer and his fellow junior officers are discussing the nature of the Navy. Keefer says, "The Navy is a master plan designed by geniuses for execution by idiots. If you are not an idiot, but find yourself in the Navy, you can only operate well by pretending to be one. All the shortcuts and economies and commonsense changes that your native intelligence suggests to you are mistakes. Learn to quash them. Constantly ask yourself, 'How would I do this if I were a fool?' Throttle down your mind to a crawl. Then you will never go wrong." I think would be safe to say that Keefer was not a fan of Navy bureaucracy. Neither was Kafka: "Every revolution evaporates and leaves behind only the slime of a new bureaucracy."

But consider this. A modern nuclear aircraft carrier is one of the most complex pieces of technology in existence. It will have a crew of over 6,000 sailors. Their average age is between 20 and 24, most with just a high school education. How could a group like this possibly operate such a complex device?

Rules and procedures developed and run by a bureaucracy.

The geniuses who *designed* the system would have tried to imagine every possible operational contingency and create a procedure that could address the exigency when it was identified. Would they be able to imagine every circumstance? No, the fog of war suggests that the outcomes of battle are not absolutely predictable.

However, the more specific the rules are for handling a complex situation, the greater the probability that a young and inexperienced operator will be able to handle it. A university, however, is a very different breed of cat, and I believe this is where many of the frustrations of older-generation faculty at the rise of bureaucracy in universities arose.

I went to college in the '60s, and as Woodstock, *Easy Rider*, and *The Organization Man* might predict, my cohorts and I were not big bureaucracy fans. Colleges offered refuge from the mind-deadening conformity that we thought awaited us in the corporate life. A college job was where you could do your own thing, and follow your creative impulses unfettered. The first couple of decades of my time at a university delivered on the promise of freedom from busywork, but we didn't think very much about the sources of revenue that permitted this intellectually idyllic life.

The '80s represented a transition decade. The relative reduction of state funding had led to the "redefinition of scholastic excellence" to continue enough revenue stream to keep the doors open. Two films came out at this time that to those of us who arrived 10–20 years before seemed to represent what was happening in universities, and what more might happen if things didn't turn around.

Michael Radford's *1984* came out in—1984. It featured a number of chilling concepts like *Newspeak*, where the meaning of words was altered to support the doctrine of the bureaucracy (scholastic excellence), or the *Memory Hole*, where physical evidence of anything contradicting the ruling party's view of history could be destroyed (failed income-generating schemes).

The following year, Terry Gilliam's bizarre dystopian *Brazil* appeared offering an even grimmer foretaste of what might happen when bureaucracies displaced all other aspects of society (like democracy).

Another fundamental change started to appear in colleges and universities that would have just as profound an effect as increasing bureaucratization, but was more complex to deal with because it seemed to represent an example of the Law of Unintended Consequences—an outcome not apparent when a plan was conceived.

Social change has been a part of America since its beginnings. However, for much of their history, colleges were largely independent of these changes, especially rapid ones, because their ivory tower status kept them isolated from the ebb and flow of social dynamics.

In the '60s this changed dramatically, and colleges became one of the major agencies of social change. Civil rights, women's rights, environment, peace activism, etc., all started to find homes in colleges. As long as these activities were primarily in the volunteer arena, there was little impact on the mainstream educational programs of the university. However, once they started to became formalized as a result of government and organizational participation, they began to have a dramatic effect on the way the college ran, especially those that were state-supported, even in areas that were remote from the topic of the social activity, largely because they started to require a part of the ever-shrinking general budget which had once largely been supplied by state governments, or in the case of private schools, tuition.

The primary reason for this seems to be that a government agency could specify, under threat of punishment, that certain things had to be done, but the agency had no obligation to FUND the changes that it mandated. To be sure, there were often government funds available, usually in the form of grants, to facilitate performance, but enforcement was executed whether funding was available or not. For example, at the time of writing there are six salaried people on the staff of the URI Environmental Health and Safety office. This office was not there before the EPA was created. A worthwhile and necessary activity? To be sure. But where do the salaries come from if there is not a dedicated outside funding source? Clearly, from traditional sources, like department teaching budgets, or campus maintenance.

So increased bureaucratization at a university means not only the frustration of extra forms to fill out, approvals to get, and workshops to attend, but a reduction in the ability to provide the central raison d'etre of a college education; a refinement of the students' ability to think.

Younger faculty I've talked to about this seem much less bothered by creeping bureaucratization than those of my generation, or even one or two generations beyond. This is probably because they've never known any other way of doing business, and have adapted—and after all, adaptation is nature's way of avoiding extinction. So I don't look for any revolutions from the younger faculty coming soon to send the bureaucrats back to their cubbyholes.

Chapter 26
How It All Began, and Where It Might be Going

For most of their existence, American colleges and universities had two main student clientele; the rich, who went to college as part of their mating game, and those who loved the life of the mind, and planned to become scholars. There were in addition specialized institutions like medical and engineering schools, and teacher's colleges. But for the mainstream—the major state universities and the more exclusive private schools, this situation was stable for decades, as was the student body.

World War II dramatically changed that. That war was one of science and technologies, and enormous resources were poured into institutions like University of Chicago (Met Lab—atomic pile), MIT (Radiation Lab—radar), and University of California, Berkeley (Rad Lab—cyclotron). When the war was over, it was clear that science and technology had played a huge role in the Allied victory, and later with the perceived rise in the threat posed by the Soviet Union, vigorous support for science and technology received high priority in what would be the expansion of college enrollments after 1946, often at the expense of the humanities and social sciences.

Much of this enrollment increase was due to the Servicemen's Readjustment Act of 1944 (GI Bill) for returning military. One of its stipulations was provision for free undergraduate tuition and expenses for GIs to attend colleges and trade schools. As a result of this postwar pulse of enrollments starting in 1946 and its accompanying rash of complaints due to overcrowding, colleges engaged in enormous expansion programs in the '50s and early '60s, both in physical plant and staffing. However, when the last of the ex-GIs graduated, there was recognition that there had been overbuilding, and something needed to be done to keep the new buildings filled, and the new faculty busy. It was about this time that the idea that "You need to go to college to get a good job" surfaced. That hadn't been true for a long time, and it really wasn't true at the time. American industry was thriving, the labor unions were still powerful, and there continued the perception that manufacturing jobs represented the best of both worlds; stability and good salaries.

However, the worm of change was beginning to burrow up through the soil of American industry. In 1950, the noted American war photographer

David Douglas Duncan was given a tour through the Japanese optical company Nippon Kogaku in Tokyo in preparation for his assignment to photograph the Korean War. Duncan used the German-made Leica camera for this kind of work, as did most of his contemporaries. The company rep showed him a new line of lenses called "Nikon" that would fit his camera and claimed that they were superior to their German counterparts. Duncan shot a roll of film, had it developed, and was stunned to see that the claim was correct. The Nikon lenses were sensational. Duncan brought the lenses to Korea and shot pictures for *Life* magazine. Stories about the superb quality of the lenses spread rapidly through the ranks of the other photographers, who carried and spread the message back to the United States. This marked the beginning of the end of the postwar perception of "cheap Japanese goods" and paved the way for other Japanese brands, like Sony, that became synonymous with high quality. In 1971, if you wanted a high quality hand-made TV set, you bought an American Zenith. Today, you get a Samsung (made mostly in Korea). Ironically, the Zenith name is today owned by the Korean LG, although sets haven't been available for several years.

The long-term result of this was that skilled manufacturing jobs, which had been highly desirable for blue-collar families now started to disappear. So what was a kid in one of those families to do? If the kid had been smart enough to be a master machinist for Kodak, he/she could be educated to be a white-collar worker, whose ranks were increasing faster than the blue-collar jobs were disappearing. So, it was about in the '80s that "you have to go to college to get a good job" began to have both truth and resonance, and a new audience for college pitches started to form.

So it appears that the rise in college bureaucracy did not have a singular cause, nor did it evolve the same way in all institutions. There does seem to be a general chronological sequence:

1. *Big pulse of returning GI's from WWII on the GI Bill, starting in 1946.*

2. *Expansion of college sciences and engineering, primarily funded by federal government, with corresponding relative decline in humanities and social sciences support.*

3. *Colleges overbuild in structures and staff to accommodate blown up post-war enrollments.*

4. After pulse of GI's graduate, realization in the '50s that non-traditional students will have to be attracted to keep the classrooms full. "You have to go to college to get a good job" begins to have some truth to it as traditional high-skill blue collar jobs start to disappear.

5. Second explosion of science and tech related funds to colleges from federal government in '60s to meet Soviet fear. State governments build up their universities in hopes of making them competitive for these funds.

6. Relatively rapid shrinkage of state funds available for development and routine running of colleges in '70s as state governments realize that competing successfully for federal funds will be more expensive than anticipated. College expenses increase dramatically as a result of overbuilding of staff and structures.

7. Full tuition out-of-staters, and grant overhead replace state funding for routine operations. Colleges begin using heterodox recruiting methods to attract non-traditional full tuition-paying students, mostly out-of-state in '80s.

8. Federal student loan programs start in a big way in late '60s and are of elephantine proportions today. Administering these programs increases campus bureaucratic load, and creates a new creature, the for-profit college.

9. Increasing workloads on tenured faculty in areas that have grants available make administrative jobs more difficult to do part time, increasing demand for full-time professional bureaucrats to staff administration jobs. Also, grant-holding faculty have less time for teaching, so adjuncts, not full-timers replace them in courses.

10. Increase in bureaucracy in agencies outside the colleges (EPA, OSHA, etc.) that impinge on college operations drives increase in bureaucracy inside. Gradual increase since '80s.

11. Incorporation of social concerns originating outside the colleges into daily college operations (diversity, women's rights, etc.) increases bureaucracy inside the college to administer official programs that formerly were informal and outside.

12. Development of a self-perpetuating, and ever increasing class of college administrators who have a different set of goals for measuring success in administration than the traditional ones, and which are sometimes in conflict with traditional faculty goals.

What we seem to be looking at is an inevitable process, following the changes in the larger society that have taken place since the end of WWII. Both sides of the political spectrum, left and right, seem to agree that colleges have gone to hell in a handbasket—but for different reasons, and with different outcomes.

As I started to come to the end of this writing sojourn, which was based on personal recollections supplemented by personal documents, I began to wonder if anybody else was thinking about the relationship between bureaucracy and day-to-day operations in colleges. After all, I'm a retiree, and haven't been involved with the routine hurly-burly of college for over a decade. However, it appears that even at present, bureaucracy in colleges is still a large issue. A quick search through Amazon Books found 26 titles published between 2008 and the present dealing with college bureaucracy, and the adoption of corporate administrative structures in colleges. There seem to be two main threads running through these books; the appearance of a large, permanent, bureaucrat class in college operation, and an increasing use of colleges to further the interests of large corporations.

So as I now prepare to return to my placid retirement life of writing railroad history books, what do I conclude from all this? First, now that there are a number of books out about college bureaucracy, either college bureaucrats have changed a lot in the last ten years, or the bureaucracy-book authors are demonizing college administrators a bit. The ones I remember from many years ago were genuine scholars who might have been in a family situation where they needed more money, or did have an idea that they could run things better than their predecessors. I found them ready to listen to argument, and whether I won or lost, I always had the feeling I could come back with a new issue, and we could start from ground zero. I also found a number of letters from administrators expressing frustration that they could not honor my requests for resources, and I believe they were honest. Maybe that's different now—I don't really know.

Now that I've been away from academia for almost a decade, I STILL think I had one of the best jobs in the world. But I have increasingly come to realize that I have that feeling because I was in the right place at the right time. Many of the things that made the job so wonderful seem to have altered, perhaps irretrievably, hopefully not so. If there is to be a return to more intellectually stimulating times, I think it is going to have to arise from faculty who have a secure enough position on campus through their outside funding and consequent mobility to challenge the entrenched bureaucrats who like things just the way they are. This will not be easy, and cannot be assured of success, but American colleges and universities were so enormously valuable to American youth and society that they should not be given up to the functionaries without a fight.

Note Added in June 2020

This book was completed as the novel Corona virus was beginning its lockdown phase in the US. It seems clear that for at least a year or two, probably more, there will be dramatic effects on colleges and universities, and almost certainly there will be an impact on the relationship of college bureaucracies to the rest of the college enterprise.

I believe the biggest change will be in the role and methodology of teaching. As classes have moved online, professors have discovered that this medium bears little relationship to the teaching methods they are accustomed to. Already, many studies have documented a cutback in students' attention spans, and the online medium as it currently exists has little ability to capture the interest of homebound students. In addition, as more and more students who do not have traditional college prep backgrounds enter college, the potential for a variety of disasters looms.

This presents an opportunity to adapt to the new reality. Large class lecturers who made imaginative use of video in their live classes were pre-adapted to be successful when they went online. Their techniques should be studied and adopted. One of the best examples I'm familiar with is Michael Sandel of Harvard, whose "Justice" course became famous in online circles. But the success record of MOOC (Massive Open Online Courses) is not encouraging. These enterprises appear to require an inordinate amount of faculty time and have a disappointing completion rate. To expect most universities to quickly adapt to a MOOC-style course format, even for smaller courses, is probably unreasonable.

So what will be the role of bureaucracies in this? I'll go out on a limb and predict that the model for bureaucracies in place now will be followed, and the bureaucracy will simply balloon. Existing full-time faculty will be so overwhelmed by the magnitude of their new tasks that they will have even less time for participation in administration than they did before. So professional administrations will become more firmly entrenched and in charge of a wider variety of enterprises. They will be difficult to dislodge when things settle down.

Is it possible that I could be wrong about this? Absolutely, and I hope so. There are still some wonderful people serving as college administrators who retain an old-fashioned and non-bureaucratic way of looking at the role and function of a college administration and I hope, for the sake of an institution I grew up with and love, that they come to prevail.

About the Author

Frank Heppner received his A.B. from the University of California, Berkeley in 1962, M.S. from San Francisco State University in 1964, and Ph.D. from the University of California, Davis in 1967. After two years of post-doctoral research at the University of Washington, he came to the University of Rhode Island and remained there until his retirement in 2010.

He taught 15 different courses at Rhode Island. His largest class was the 960-student Biology 2, and over his career he taught over 25,000 students. He was an active researcher, and had over 50 publications, many in the leading journals in his field. Toward the end of his career, he developed an interest in the profession of college teaching, and wrote a number of papers on the subject, and several books.

He was active in university administration, serving terms as Chair of the Department of Biological Sciences, and director of the Honors program. He traveled extensively, and had Fulbright Fellowships in the Philippines and Borneo.

He also participated heavily in community service, being at various times the chair of the local conservation commission and public housing authority. He was one of the founding members of the Friends of the Kingston Station, an historic preservation group, and was a squadron commander of the Rhode Island Civil Air Patrol.

In retirement, he builds model ships, and several of his models are in museums in Rhode Island and New York.

Professor Frank Heppner in the character of Prof. Dr. Viktor Alucard, preparing for a lecture on the biological basis of myth and legend. Picture taken 1975.